safe from the
madness

The three people who kept me safe from the madness:
my grandparents, Alex and Alice, and my mother, Simone.
We are on a summer outing during the war.

safe from the
madness

A MEMOIR

FRANÇOISE WEBB

Safe from the Madness
A Memoir

Second edition.

ISBN: 978-1979447553

Printed in the United States of America

In loving memory of
my grandparents, Alex and Alice
my mother, Simone

And in honor of
my mentor, Arthur

Acknowledgements

My grateful thanks to my friends: Elizabeth Moisan for her incredible input in the fine editing, the book design, and her unique creative talent in designing the cover; Marjorie Frith for copy editing a major portion of the original manuscript; Jacqueline Loring, whose writing class first relit my spark; Christie Lowrance for her guidance through first drafts of early stories; Dr. Frances Nenna for offering valuable suggestions; Tara Champy, whose loyal support showed in her generous contribution of time and effort in preparing the final manuscript; and to Sharon Blair, who volunteered to read my manuscript aloud to me.

Thanks to the members of the Harwich Rising Tide Writers and the now-dispersed Sandwich Library writers group who, for the last eight years, listened and encouraged me to dig deeper into the past. And to the following members of the Rising Tide Writers: Theodore Shrady, Barbara Leedom, Sebastian Mudry, Ingrid Stabins, Rachel Crosby and Ed

Cottier. A special thanks to Bill and Jan Richmond for showing me a new path.

In honor of my mentor, Arthur, whose steadfast belief, encouragement and support enabled me to complete this arduous, exciting eight-year endeavor.

And in grateful, fond memory of Chip Bishop, *New York Times* best-selling author, for the powerful praise that fueled my writing.

Author's Notes

French Commander Emile Arthur Soudart, my great-grandfather, in chapter five, The Blue Letter, was Head of La Section du Chiffre, assigned to Le Grand Quartier Général during The First World War.

Alexandre Jules Bendelé, my maternal grandfather, I call him Papy in my book, was a French Army officer in WWI. He fought with his men in the trenches before being captured and held prisoner for more than three years in Germany. He escaped and walked to the Holland border, returning to Paris to his wife and daughter, my mother.

Kommandantur. Official German Police Centers assigned to different precincts throughout occupied villages and cities. They commandeered local police stations. People brought in for interrogation were often tortured there before being taken away.

The Gestapo Headquarters, 347 Avenue Louise, Brussels, was not far from my "magical woods", the Bois de la

Cambre. The Secret Police of Nazi Germany, the Gestapo was founded by Hermann Goering, but run by Heinrich Himmler. Their goal was terrorizing and intimidating the population. They were originally Hitler's personal bodyguards.

The SS symbol stands for "Schutzstaffel" (Protection Squadron), the elite Aryan military branch. Under Himmler's direction, the SS carried out Hitler's "Final Solution", and administered the Nazi concentration camp system.

The Wehrmacht was Germany's regular military force, composed of the army, navy, and air force. The headquarters in Brussels was at 155 Rue de la Loi.

Odile Henri Ovart was a teacher, then director of my school, *Lycée Gatti de Gamond*. A member of a Secret Army, she sheltered ten Jewish children inside the school's boarding section. Following a denunciation and a raid, she was deported to Bergen-Belsen concentration camp in Germany, where she died of typhoid fever. In 1994 her memory was honored with *The Righteous Among the Nations* award. In school, we were not told the truth about her disappearance and death.

The stylized flower at the end of the epilogue is the yellow iris, the symbol of the City of Brussels.

"Les souvenirs sont nos forces."
Souvenirs are our strength.
Victor Hugo

"Life breaks us and afterwards many are
strong at the broken places."
Ernest Hemingway

Contents

Introduction

As a rapid barrage of bombs fell, a sharp white light hit the basement again, yet I couldn't see anything. Oh, where did everyone go? My grandparents? And where was Juliette?

It was the flash of light that confused me. For in the basement deep beneath our building, where we sought refuge, there were no windows. I heard new explosions as bombs hit another target.

That light. Where was that light coming from? Had we been hit this time? I peered at my grandfather, but even in this semi-dark, I knew he was next to my grandmother, close to her. Curled up on a bench next to them, I snuggled closer to my grandmother. She felt soft as a pillow. For an instant, I caught a slight familiar scent. Verbena. Her favorite fragrance.

Another blast shook the room. Trembling I reached for the scratchy blue blanket, the one we brought with us when we ran down to our shelter in the basement at night. It was there over me, now it was gone. I tried to reach my grandmother, but she too was gone.

"Grand-mère! Grand-père! Where are you?" I looked around me. "Juliette! Juliette!" No one answered.

More bombs! Screaming, exploding, destroying, they fell. The light again! So close. Then I understood. Tonight, it was our building, our lives. *Ah, oui,* tonight, we were their target.

There was a square of light across from my bench where the wall had been. I was alone.

Again, left all alone. Short of breath, I sat up, my heart rapidly beating. A tear on my face ran down upon my neck.

In the distance, the rumble of thunder echoed again as the summer storm passed. A weak flash of lightning brightened my window, silhouetting the hanging fern. A fresh night breeze blew into my bedroom, billowing gauzy curtains. A moment later, playful raindrops pattered upon the window sill. I pushed back the soft duvet cover, got out of bed and closed the window.

Will it always be like this? So many thunderstorms, in so many places I've lived since my childhood in Nazi occupied Brussels have often brought me the same dream filled with fright. A dream of bombs then darkness, a dream of comfort then fear, a dream of eternity and abrupt endings, a dream of being alive and of loss. I remember feeling these things as a child and war raged around us. I lived with my grandparents in an elegant apartment building from where I could watch my beloved Brussels. This was "our nest." Our own cocoon.

Our own peaceful shelter.

My grandfather, Papy, had experienced the ravages of war as a French army officer in World War I, The Great War, "The War to End All War."

My grandmother, Mamie, the daughter of a highly decorated French Army Commander, was raised with military discipline which produced her strong, stoic character.

My mother. Early in life, she, too learned lessons of survival, when as a young child, not knowing if her father was being killed in battle, as she spent nights filled with fear huddled with her mother in a Paris basement while German bombs rained from above.

Of course, now I am alone, for the ones who filled my life with their unending love are long gone. Many years have passed since my childhood days. Many years since Nazi soldiers took people away in those green trucks. And so many years for me to learn the true history of the insanity that poisoned the world and forced itself into our lives. So many years to remember, understand, and cherish the memory of those who kept me safe from the madness.

The Parade
Late August 1942

Unaware this was to be the last Saturday I would live with my parents, I stood in their bedroom in front of their mirrored armoire and admired my reflection.

Emilie, my nanny, quickly buttoned my blue-flowered summer dress. "you are a very lucky girl," she said, tying the sash in a bow at the back. "*Oui, petite,* you are going to the boulevard. *Oui,* now you are going to see a real Belgian parade after all."

I asked, "Are we going together?"

"*Ah, non, petite,*" she smiled. "This morning you're going with your Maman and your Papa. Now let's hurry." She brushed my short, dark hair, then combed my bangs with a wet comb.

From one of my mother's perfume bottles on the dresser, she dabbed a drop of cologne behind my ears. "*Et voila.* Now, go, *vite, ma petite.*"

I ran toward my parents waiting in the foyer and at

once sensed the familiar, uncomfortable tension between them. I noticed the annoyed expression on my father's face. He shook his head and turned away from me as the dining room clock rang those endless, Westminster chimes. His voice was abrupt. "*Alors*, then let's go."

My mother smiled. She took my hand. "*Ah, oui*, and here we are, the three of us. All together."

There was a moment of surprising contrast as we left the dark, coolness of the grey marble lobby behind and stepped into the dazzling August sunlight. I enjoyed walking between them, the warmth of the late morning sun on my body felt good. It made me happy, but after four or five blocks our pace accelerated, and I could not keep up with my father's long strides.

My mother whispered, "Just try walking a little faster," but I couldn't, and sensed my father's growing annoyance as he walked ahead of us. We turned onto a side street.

"There's half an hour before the parade starts," he said, and stopped at the familiar shop of his regular wine merchant. He stepped down and entered the dark, sour smelling shop. We lingered behind, but then followed.

"Perhaps you should wait until after the parade?" suggested my mother. But he ignored her, and with great care was already selecting his new choices of wines for the week. The owner, a balding, serious looking man with glasses, had some new arrivals to recommend. He repeatedly adjusted his glasses as they both read labels and discussed the various merits of each. I stood next to my mother, and waited with growing anticipation.

My father paid for his selection while the bottles were being placed in a large, sturdy bag. "I will return to pick these up after the parade."

With the faint sounds of marching bands in the distance, my father pulled me aside. He leaned down and whispered, "You stay here and *sois sage*, be good. Just wait for us here." He turned away, grabbed my mother's bare arm with firm determination, and led her out of the shop. She never looked back. I was stunned. This was a mistake. Surely my mother was going to come back, and the three of us would see the parade together as planned. I waited. I watched the door, and waited.

The door suddenly opened, but it was not my mother. It was a man. A customer. He spoke to the merchant about certain wines he wanted to purchase. The merchant glared at me and pointed. "Go sit on that crate, in the corner. And don't move."

The man, amused by my lone presence in the shop, inquired how and why I was there. The merchant gave him an explanation, but he was annoyed and shook his head in disbelief. The man smirked and carrying his purchases left the shop. I still believed my mother would return, but as sounds of marching bands grew louder, **my** last flicker of hope disappeared. Now, sitting all alone, I understood.

This was no mistake. I had purposely been left behind. She was not coming back. Both were at the parade, enjoying it without me. My insides felt empty.

Because I visited the wine shop before with my father, I knew where Boulevard Anspach was from here. Half a block away, at the end of this short street.

I stood, but the wine merchant shook his finger and spoke in a sharp voice. "Sit there. Don't move." He climbed on a step-ladder and re-arranged his stock along the wooden racks lining the walls, so high they reached the brown ceiling of his musty shop. From the tone of his voice and the annoyed look he gave me, I knew he did not want me here. I sat down and devised a plan for my escape.

I knew that the narrow door was awkward for people to enter. This slowed customers as they maneuvered the curved wooden steps and held on to the frail metal railing while stepping down into the shop. My plan turned into action when two customers opened the door and, cautiously, stepped down the stairs. I seized the moment and bolted. Running through their legs I knocked one off balance. The angry wine merchant shouted, "Catch her, quick! Bring that kid back!"

One of the prospective customers tried, but was so startled he missed me. Running away, I looked back once as he stared in disbelief. I ran as fast as I could toward the boulevard. Ducking into small groups of people walking to the parade, I blended in. I was free.

While sitting on the wine crate, I had figured out how to find my parents. Since they arrived early, they would be on the sidewalk in the front row near the boulevard, and because they were taller than average, especially my father, I would easily spot the tops of their heads above the rest of the crowd. All I needed to do was work my way to the curb. Being small, I managed to squeeze my way through the standing spectators. At times, I unfortunately stepped on a foot which made the person jump, leaving me a space to move ahead. The crowd was six to eight people deep, but soon I broke free and stood in the front row as the first band marched toward me. I had not missed the parade!

Now I needed to find my parents. I ran into the middle of the boulevard and turned to look for my father's black-striped suit jacket and my mother's turquoise summer dress. But I was in the path of the oncoming band, and people shouted for me to step back. Just as I caught a glimpse of my father's head and a fragment of bright turquoise blue, I was grabbed and pulled out of the way. I yanked myself free, then ran, calling, "Papa, Papa, I'm here!"

Spectators stared at me, a young child finding her missing parents in this crowd. My father said, "I told you to stay in the shop and wait for us. How did you get here?"

"But, you couldn't have found us by yourself," my mother wondered. "*Alors*, just tell me, who did you come with?"

I tried to tell them, but a band was marching by. My

voice could not be heard. I did not care. I was enjoying the festive sights and loud music, while around us spectators were excited by Belgian workers being allowed to parade, holding their Guilds' banners and large, colorful flags. Today, these men and women were marching, proud not only of their crafts, but proud to march as Belgian citizens in their own country. They exuded national pride and the crowd responded with loud, encouraging cheers. To keep the people back, only a few soldiers slowly rode by along the side of the boulevard on their green German motorcycles with sidecars. Wearing goggles, they looked like huge, ugly, slow-moving toads. As they passed by, a few brave, defiant spectators, scattered in the back of the crowd, shouted insults. Others only dared to murmur in agreement.

I had a clear view of everything since we stood on the curb in the front row. I waved at people marching. Some waved back. A lady whispered to the man marching next to her. He smiled and nodded. "*Bonjour, ma mignonne,*" she said, as she handed me a flower from her red bouquet, then ran back to her spot next to the man.

"*Merci,* Madame" I whispered.

"Ah, what a pretty flower," my mother said. "How nice! It's called a carnation. Aren't you a lucky girl?"

This rare Belgian celebration lasted a long time and people were pleased. When the crowd dispersed the three of us headed home, but first we stopped by the wine shop, so my father could pick up his morning's purchase. I refused to go in and my mother stayed outside with me. She leaned back against the iron railing and smiled. "Why don't you stand over here next to me, and face the sun? *Mais oui*, come, let's enjoy these rays of sunshine together."

But I did not want to. I did not understand why, but it was no longer the same. She seemed different now, like my father, and I no longer felt secure with them. I stood alone, inhaling small, delicate whiffs of the red flower called carnation and decided I would bring it to Emilie. She loved red.

The shop door re-opened. The wine merchant followed my father outside. He held his glasses and spoke a warning. "Don't ever step inside my shop again." He glanced at my mother then shook his head in disgust.

As we headed home my mother asked, "But what happened?"

My father gave a small, harsh laugh. He shrugged. "Oh, nothing. He just did not think it was a nice thing to do to one's child. That's all."

During our absence, Emilie prepared lunch. She was getting ready to serve it in the dining room, when, tired and confused, I tugged at the back of her apron. "I want to eat with you in the kitchen," I whispered. "I want to sit with you please, not my parents." It felt safer.

It was in the kitchen, during our lunch together, a glass with the red carnation between us, that Emilie asked, "So, *ma petite*, tell me all about the parade." And I did.

Three days later, with Emilie's help, fate chose to intervene on my behalf. After my parents left for work that Tuesday morning, I sat perched high upon their large, velvet covered bed, and played with my new doll, while Emilie packed most of our clothes and a few of my toys. After we shared our customary lunch, we left. She carried the large brown suitcase and I carried my doll. We walked hand-in-hand down the street to my waiting grandparents' nearby apartment, singing our favorite song *"Il Etait Un Petit Navire."* There Once Was a Little Ship.

But I was much too young to understand the magnitude of this moment. This short walk led me to the beginning of an adventure-filled period in my childhood, in the safety of my grandparents' sun-filled, top-floor apartment, later to be referred to as "our nest." There, embraced with the love of doting, wise and protective grandparents, I survived the years of World War II in Nazi-occupied Brussels.

Un Vrai Miracle
December 1942 - May 1943

Before my fourth birthday, my nanny Emilie left us to return to Liège and care for her mother. Promising to return for regular visits, she departed our tenth-floor nest. A new nanny, Madame Luytens was hired, but she would spend only the days with us. Since she lived six blocks away, it worked out well.

At this point I knew about *"Le Petit Jésus,"* Little Jesus who watched over me at all times, and because I visited many of Brussels' beautiful old churches with my grandfather and Emilie, I had a notion of the possibility of miracles. Certain saints were more gifted than others in accomplishing these feats, but I knew, if one prayed hard enough, miracles could happen without going all the way to Lourdes.

Madame Luytens, my new nanny, wore black from head to toe: shoes, stockings, skirt, blouse. The only exception was a pair of brown plaid wool slippers she wore in our apartment and the blue smock left by Emilie. I often saw her dab her eyes as she folded my clothes, or prepared my lunch, and I was sad for her. I liked her.

One day, as she was putting things away, I noticed tears in her eyes and asked her, "Why? Why are you so sad?"

She explained her beloved husband Jules had gone to war three years ago and, after a long silence, she received news he probably had been killed in an early battle near the town of Maestricht. "Nothing truly final, you understand, *ma petite*."

Alas, I understood her tears. She missed her husband Jules and wanted him back. As she took out her bright blue wallet and showed me his photograph, she wiped her eyes. He had dark hair, a mustache and stood holding a bicycle in a country setting. "That was a beautiful day in May, an entire day spent together in the countryside."

I gave her a kiss on the cheek and felt both relieved and special to have been taken into her confidence regarding her grief, her *gros chagrin*. From that day on, I made an effort and tried to be kind to her and to behave when she asked me to. I even told her about the saints in the church and of burning a candle for special requests. That same afternoon, we walked to Sainte Catherine's and both of us lit a candle for Jules' return.

Months passed. Madame Luytens no longer cried and we got on very well. After all, I was her friend and every day after lunch we went out for a promenade. "For fresh air and sunshine," said my grandmother.

I loved our afternoons together. Hand-in- hand, we walked to my nearby park and on sunny days I took my

In the park with Madame Luytens.

doll in her carriage so that she, too, could have "fresh air and sunshine." Often, Madame Luytens agreed to play ball or hopscotch with me. In her black purse she carried a paper bag filled with colored chalks. We drew flowers on the pavement next to my favorite bench, where later, we shared afternoon snacks and fed the sparrows and pigeons with our leftovers. Other days, we walked along Rue de Flandre, stopping to admire the displays in store windows, discussing and pointing at the items we liked best, and why. After lighting our two candles in Sainte Catherine Church for Jules' return, we often purchased fresh fruits from the outdoor market, which Madame Luytens allowed me to sample during our leisurely walk back home. Life was good.

One afternoon, instead of our usual direction, Madame Luytens chose a different street and headed the opposite way. I recognized the street, because Chez Antoine's hair salon was nearby. I often accompanied my mother and grandmother there. Even I had my hair cut there.

"But — Madame, are we going to Chez Antoine for a haircut?"

"Ah *non, non, ma petite*, we are not going to Chez Antoine," she replied, shaking her head, smiling. Instead, we entered a low, stone apartment building directly across the street. She had a key and seemed familiar with the surroundings. We walked up two flights of cold terrazzo stairs, and again, using her own key, she unlocked the door to a small, neat apartment. "This, this is *mon chez-moi*, my own place," she said. I was flattered to be invited to her home. Once our shoes were removed and our sweaters hung, she busied herself in the tiny kitchen to make us hot chocolate. I heard the familiar sound of tin boxes being taken down from cupboards and I knew cookies would be served.

Walking to the large front window and pushing back the lace curtain, I saw the familiar sign, Chez Antoine. "Madame, might there be an appointment for a haircut later on?" I asked once more.

"*Mais non. Non, ma petite.*"

Relieved, I enjoyed trying out the large, comfortable sofa, the big club chair, and admired her pretty violets by the window. I made a tour of the apartment, even used the bathroom. We had our own small feast, of assorted cookies and delicious hot chocolate. After I selected a paper wrapped bonbon from a fluted, red glass dish, Madame Luytens suggested I might enjoy a little nap on the sofa before leaving for our afternoon promenade.

Right now a nap sounded good to me. A pillow with a freshly ironed, white linen pillowcase was produced, and as a light pink blanket neatly folded in half was gently placed over me she explained, "I will be doing some light ironing in the bedroom, *ma petite*. We will leave whenever you wake up."

I felt warm and quite safe, *très contente*, very happy. The pillowcase had a faint, clean, scent of lavender, and I really liked that. Yet another pleasant thing.

As I felt my eyes close, I noticed a large, ornate frame

with a photograph of Monsieur Jules Luytens in his military uniform and his dark mustache. A wide, black crepe ribbon was draped diagonally over the frame. Remembering that, I had included the request in my nightly prayers that Monsieur Luytens would find his way back into Madame Luytens' empty arms. Drifting off to sleep, I now concluded that this was, after all, a very nice place for him to come home to. *Très, très, comfortable.*

I must have slept quite a while because, when I awoke, the sun no longer shone through the front window. Evening was approaching. I moved the curtain aside and noticed that across the street at Chez Antoine, lights were being turned off, one by one. I tip-toed to the table for another bonbon. Slowly, I then realized complete silence filled the apartment. I called for Madame Luytens.

"*Ah, ah, oui.* Just a moment, *ma petite.*" She sounded sleepy. I could smell pipe tobacco, just like my father's. After knocking politely on the bedroom door, I opened it on my own. There, in the big bed, under the covers, was Madame Luytens with a man. They both seemed very happy and invited me to come in. She said, "*Ma petite,* this is my husband."

I nearly fainted. I was delirious with joy. My nightly prayers had worked. Awed by *un vrai miracle,* a true miracle, I approached the edge of the bed on tiptoes then, gently touched his hand.

"I am so happy you found your way back from the war. Your wife really missed you. But — where is your mustache?"

He smiled, but said nothing. Leaning toward his left, he picked up his pipe from a round, pink, floral ashtray on the night stand, then with obvious pleasure, he slowly re-lit it.

Suddenly, Madame Luytens re-appeared with our sweaters and shoes. The lights at Chez Antoine had all been turned off. We hastened home, along the dark, narrow cobblestone Rue du Grand-Serment.

"Ah, *oui*, very good. Just in time. Oh, and how was your afternoon promenade *ma petite chérie?*" asked my grandmother.

"*Superbe!*" I replied, as Madame Luytens exited quickly, while putting her index finger upon her lips.

That night, in the middle of supper, I could no longer stand not sharing the incredible news. I waited until Augustine, our maid, cleared the soup bowls and served the main course. Suddenly I exclaimed, "This afternoon, *un vrai miracle* has taken place right here among us." My heart raced as I waited for their response.

"*Un miracle, ma petite?* What do you mean?" my grandfather asked. This was the moment I had been waiting for since the soup course. And out it all came. The various saints, the many candles we lit in different churches during our promenades and, of course, my nightly prayers, sometimes even under the covers once in my bed, and now — "*Un vrai miracle.*"

I held the attention of everyone at the table. My mother was the first, but, one by one, they put their forks down. All eyes were upon me. Even the dour Augustine stood in the doorway, wiping her hands on her apron, listening to my every word.

Deliberately, I slowly dropped the bombshell.

"Monsieur Jules, the husband of Madame Luytens, is alive and has returned home from the war. *Ah, oui. Un vrai miracle.* Truly!"

I thought my news would make them happy, but they told me it was, unfortunately, an impossibility. I held my ground.

"How can you not believe me? And besides, I have just seen him. I touched his arm. He even smokes a pipe like Papa."

Instantly, the mood changed. Augustine crossed herself then sadly shook her head in disbelief. After certain looks were exchanged among the family, I was slowly coaxed to describe my afternoon from the beginning, from the moment we left the apartment after lunch, until our return, forty-five minutes ago.

Madame Luytens was dismissed the next day. I never understood why we were not allowed to say goodbye. But, all in all, I did not feel badly, because I knew she was once again happy with her husband Jules in that cozy little apartment across the street from Chez Antoine.

A Desolate House
January 1943 – October 1945

Madame Schroeder was tall, British, and wore a wig. I knew this because I overheard my mother and Mamie discuss that Mabel's perfectly coiffed hair was "*une perruque.*"

Monsieur and Madame Schroeder, once neighbors of my grandparents, still lived in Tervueren. Mabel was one of the ladies who sometimes came for afternoon tea in our tenth-floor nest. She and Mamie enjoyed English conversations while they sipped scalding cups of Ceylon tea poured by Mamie from her copper samovar.

Before starting her teaching career as professor of literature at a Lycée in Paris, my grand-mère's father sent her to London to learn more English. Two days before returning home, on an impulse, she spent the last of her meager funds to purchase the Art Nouveau English brass and copper samovar she had long admired in the display window of a fancy London tea-shop. Now, years later, filled with memories of her stay in England, it was her prized possession and she carefully prepared tea in it for afternoons spent with close friends.

This afternoon tea ceremony was familiar, and I watched her detailed preparations around the table. Mamie used only her best starched lace linen tea-cloths and small napkins, her delicate Chinese porcelain cups, the polished silver spoons, the ornate creamer and the sugar bowl, half-filled with precious, rationed sugar cubes, the silver tongs alongside. Cookies or slices of pound cake and perfectly thin lemon slices set on a small dish graced the table. Sometimes, she served a thin apple tart. I enjoyed not only the aroma of the steaming, dark tea, but my grand-mère's delight as she poured the fragrant liquid from her British samovar for her guests. Her friends brought flowers which added welcome color to our surroundings. Often, I was offered a trinket or a new book. I looked forward to these afternoons, though eventually going back to my room since lengthy conversations bored me.

One day, something felt different. When I returned to the salon, Mabel and Mamie, now seated together on the settee, at once became silent. Yet, Mabel was agitated. She quickly turned away to dab her eyes. Mamie's face was red, her eyes teary. What happened? What could be wrong?

Mabel stood. Her face taut, she adjusted her scarf, gathered her purse, then explained it was time to leave. Her two tram rides to Tervueren were long, way across

Brussels. Due to the black-out, she then faced the five-minute walk to her house, alone in the dark, with only a flashlight.

Mamie blurted, "Non, non, Mabel, *la petite* and I will walk you to the tram stop. Under these circumstances, it is important. I want to see you safely on board. *Oui. Mais oui, ma chère amie*, I insist."

During our fast walk along Rue Sainte Catherine, both women spoke English in hushed tones. Unfamiliar with any evening shopping, I darted quick, curious glances inside crowded, dimly-lit shops. At times I was lucky enough to catch glimpses of meager holiday decorations still displayed in windows on this bleak January night.

We reached the crowded tram stop next to La Bourse Department Store. At five-thirty it was already crowded with workers, eager to return home. They shoved one another, at times using their elbows to gain a space ahead. Fearful of being swept away into this flowing mass of grown-ups, I held on to the side of Mamie's coat. When her tram rolled up, Mabel lingered long enough to kiss us goodbye, then allowed herself to be shoved forward into the crowded tram. She constantly adjusted her trench-coat collar, now turned up around her face.

Moments before, while whispering to Mamie, she pulled her wide-brimmed felt hat with those two green feathers down so far, I could hardly see her face. Why was she hiding? We wrenched ourselves free from the surging crowd to stand a few steps away.

It seemed odd when Mabel, once on board, chose to remain standing in the cold, on the tram's outside platform. And why did she turn away from other passengers? Yet, as her tram rolled away, she managed to wave her final discreet goodbye. My grand-mère quickly wiped away her tears.

"But, Mamie, you're crying. What's wrong?"

"Oh, *ma chérie, hélas, oui*. You see, Mabel will not be coming to see us for a while."

"But, why?"

"Well you see, the Schroeders are leaving for London."

"Why?"

"London is safer for them, *ma chérie*."

"So, will Mabel go visit the King and Queen? And watch the palace guards with those tall hats? Will they ever come back to Brussels?"

She held back a sob but did not reply.

"But, Mamie, if you please, answer me. Will Mabel ever come to tea again?"

"Oh, but *ma pauvre petite, Mon Dieu*, but how could I possibly know?"

Once back in our nest, I ran to the salon to retrieve my new book. An envelope lay on the table, a set of three keys left alongside.

Augustine was busy in the kitchen with supper preparations when Mamie insisted that tonight she should leave as soon as the meal was served. A puzzled Augustine agreed, and went back to the stove shaking her head.

During supper that evening, a vase with Mabel's red tulips centered on the table, Mamie, her voice trembling, spoke for quite a while. It was too complicated to follow. Besides, I was trying to eat those slippery strands of spaghetti. Once excused, I ran to my room to share the picture book Mabel brought me with my doll Suzette, and Teddy.

That night was the first time I heard my grandfather so angry. Why was he mad at Mamie? What had she done?

I tip-toed to the door. Everyone sounded upset. All talking at once. Repeating same words. Mabel, Monsieur Schroeder. Partners. Resign. Names. Hitler. *Les Juifs*, the Jews. The SS. Unsafe. *Les Juifs* taken away. *Grand danger. Impossible.* SS informers. *Partout, partout,* everywhere.

Mamie insisted, "Help the Schroeders. Keys. Their house. Her jewelry. A promise."

Papy shouted, "Ah, *non*, Alice. Great risk. *Non.* I forbid it!"

My mother repeated, "*Non, non* Maman. *Très dangereux* now. Unknown. House sequestered. Followed. *Absolument,* must wait."

I heard their chairs when they all stood, and at once ran to my room.

I saw those keys again, that springtime day, when my grand-mère and I rode two different trams to visit the house in Tervueren. The Schroeder's house.

From the moment we boarded our first tram, I felt uneasy. My grandmother hardly spoke. I wondered, why travel such a distance to an empty house? The Schroeders were far away in London. Why this mysterious visit?

We held hands and walked in silence a block from Avenue de Tervueren along a pleasant, but deserted, residential side street. Its brick sidewalks were lined at long intervals with thin, newly planted saplings. Mounds of crude dark soil around their base gave off a strange, powerful smell I had never experienced before. Mamie called it, "*L'engrais,* manure. It will protect these young trees and help them grow."

Within minutes, we reached the town-house with the glossy black door. Its fierce English lion's head, door-knocker still guarded the house. And today, as always, it scared me. "Mamie, I don't think we should go in. No one is here. Are you sure Mabel wants us visiting while they're away?"

She did not answer, handed me her purse, then began an agitated struggle with all three keys to find the proper one for each lock. But, only after she tried twisting the smaller top key back and forth several times, did the lock finally release its bolt with a reluctant click.

For an instant I caught a glare of disapproval in the lion's eyes as I ducked behind Mamie to follow her into the spacious, dim foyer. At once, with trembling hands, she bolted the door behind us, then quickly tucked that just-loosened strand of hair back in her chignon.

The house held a mystique for me in its Englishness.

I liked being there. It was different from what I knew.

It was cool inside. And still. Very still. The force of a silence now trapped within these walls felt powerful. Overwhelming. The hall clock remained in the corner, but its heart-beat had stopped at ten to two. When? How long had it waited for someone to wind it, so its pendulum could, once again, swing back and forth as it was supposed to? The once imposing clock, now silent, stood forlorn, abandoned, alone in the corner.

"Alors, ma chérie, don't touch anything," my grandmother warned. "Just come with me." In the desolate house, the furniture covered with white sheets, resembled scary, menacing, odd-shaped ghosts. The nearest one, in particular scared me. "Oh, but that's Monsieur Schroeder's club chair," Mamie explained, before she walked out to the hallway.

Alone in the salon, I looked for the piano, but it had been moved with other furniture to the rear of the room. I recognized its wide flat surface and one of its legs, set on a wheel, showing from beneath a sheet. Afraid of being grabbed by these ghostly threatening forms, I stepped away and tried to remember that day.

Monsieur Schroeder's birthday. The opened terrace doors. Scent of lilacs brought by warm breezes into this sunlit room. Mabel played the piano and sang English songs. Grown-ups smiled. Afterward some smoked cigars. My mother looked pretty in her blue dress. A chocolate cake. Tiny candles. Sip of champagne. Bubbles tickled my nose. A nap, next to Mamie, on that deep velvet sofa, nestled amidst those pretty colors of Mabel's needlepoint pillows.

Today, surrounded by the powerful eerie stillness permeating throughout the house, I soon felt unwell. I yearned to go outside, for sunshine, fresh air. I walked to the French doors and parted the drapes to peek at the long, walled-in garden below.

Mamie had started up the next stairs when I asked, "May I play outside?"

"*Mais oui.* A good idea, but we won't be here long. And please, *chérie*, play quietly. Do not draw the attention of neighbors. You must *absolument*, remain *très discrète*."

In the garden, I ran back and forth a few times along the two gravel alleys, then searched for the box turtle, hoping it was hiding, as it often did, somewhere beneath those dark shrubs.

But, I never found it. Perhaps Mabel placed it in her purse, and the turtle now lived in London.

Bathed in sunlight, now *très contente*, I walked to two trellises attached alongside the high brick wall looking for those sweet, tiny pears, Monsieur Schroeder's favorites. When high above me, from the other side of the wall, a man's head appeared. For an instant, I caught sight of a red face, beneath a floppy, white garden hat. I heard, "*Sacrebleu!*" then the man disappeared. Only the top of a ladder, propped against the other side of the wall remained visible.

Startled, then frightened, I ran back inside.

Mamie looked up, then quickly tucked a package wrapped in newspaper, deep into her purse, "Ah, *voila*, there you are!"

As soon as I told Mamie about the man on the ladder, her face changed. I sensed her fear. "*Et bien*, now it's time for us to leave *ma petite*. Please use the bathroom at the top of the stairs before we leave. *Voila*. Now hurry. Go. *Vite, vite*."

In the stairwell, prints of British Royal vessels remained displayed, propped as usual along a ledge, while in the corner stood the forbidden toy. A stuffed, life-sized, black English Bulldog I was never allowed to play with, nor even touch. Today, it stared back, centimeters from my reach. At long last I could touch it, even perhaps take it down. Play with it for a few moments as I had yearned to so many times. No one was around. The Schroeders were far across the sea. Mamie was in the salon. This was my chance. No one would ever know. I stared at its face. Then, stood on my toes to reach for it, when it suddenly lost its appeal. His black and white, glass button eyes were empty, vacant, void. Not like my own Teddy's warm brown eyes, back at home. Freed from the English Bulldog's spell, I ran down the rest of the steps.

"*Voila*, Mamie, I'm here."

Moments later I whispered, "*Au revoir*" to the silent hall clock, but chose to ignore the lion's head as Mamie locked the black door and at a brisk pace, led me away from the desolate house. We just reached Avenue de Tervueren, when she declared, "Let's sit on this bench."

"Here? But why?"

"Well, it's simply *nécessaire. Et voila.* That's it."

She handed me a cookie, took a book from her purse, opened it and began to read. But, why read a book on this hard, uncomfortable bench along this deserted avenue? Why did we pass by the tram stop? And besides, Mamie was not reading. She was only pretending while she darted glances back toward the direction we had walked from.

We were sitting on our second bench, when two people approached. A rare thing on this empty avenue.

"Now *petite*," Mamie warned in a whisper, "don't say anything. Just sit still. Right here. Next to me, until they've walked a good distance away."

She handed me another cookie. Only when the two passersby, a man and a woman, disappeared from view, did we resume our endless walk.

Loud motorcycles roared down the avenue followed by four or five German army trucks. With tarps rolled up, those feared green trucks were filled with Nazi soldiers. They sat across from each other with rifles held against their chests. As they rumbled passed us, I clutched Mamie's arm and looked away.

By the time we sat on our third bench, I was tired and discouraged that we let so many yellow trams pass us by.

"But, Mamie, why did we go to the house? Why was that man staring over the wall? Can't we take a tram now?"

She hesitated, then replied in a stern voice, "Now that's enough, Françoise. Please don't ask me again."

It was then we heard laughter. Her face froze. She gripped her purse against her as two Nazi soldiers, rifles strapped over their shoulders walked side-by-side and passed behind our bench while sharing a joke. When the taller one glanced at me, I thought they would stop. Mamie held her breath. Frightened, I kept quiet until both soldiers walked away. They never looked back.

She crossed herself. "Oh, *Mon Seigneur!* Oh, *la, la.* Oh, *Mon Seigneur! Dieu Merci!*" She dabbed her eyes, then whispered as she stroked my hair. "But, *ma pauvre petite, non,* oh, *non,* you just wouldn't understand." She then sighed, "Ah, let's go now, *ma chérie.*"

Once we reached the roundabout, while we waited for our tram, my grandmother darted glances at waiting passengers around us. Was she afraid of something? Or someone? I was surprised and disappointed when we did not climb aboard this awaiting tram. For at the last moment, she hesitated, turned, then mumbled, "*Non. Non, ma petite,* stay here. Let's wait for the next one."

"Why Mamie? I'm tired. I want to go home."

She remained still, while watching everyone who passed us by.

"*Eh, alors,* are you coming or not?" shouted the conductor.

She shook her head, "*Non, merci. Non.* Go ahead."

He shrugged, then tapped the floor bell twice with his foot. The familiar clanking sound of the bell was followed by wincing sounds of metal wheels moving once again along the track, the tram rolled away from the curb.

She smiled. "*Et bien, ma chérie*, now we can safely go home. *Oui*, let us go home now. This has been a most successful visit. Tomorrow, I will write the good news to Mabel. *Oui*, the house remains just as they left it. For now, everything is still safe. *Ah, oui, Dieu Merci!*" I held her hand, but still did not understand.

During our ride home aboard the next tram, I settled in a window seat, overwhelmed by Mamie's strange behavior, the scary red-faced man and today's sadness inside the Schroeder's house. I leaned my head against the window. Longing to be back safe in our nest, hold Teddy, then wait for Papy to come home, I closed my eyes and dozed off.

Months after the war, on a balmy October day, Mabel returned to our nest to once again enjoy afternoon tea with my grand-mère.

I was busy opening Mabel's present, while a beaming Mamie led her friend to our balcony and pointed to a potted red geranium. "*Voila*. It's all safe. *Mais oui, mon amie, oui*. Right in there."

Soon after, I was sent to play in my room with my new English paper dolls. I was unaware both women returned to the terrace to retrieve the sealed package. It was the one Mamie had tucked in her purse that day, brought home, then at once safely hid inside a tea cannister wrapped in oil-cloth and buried in that oversized clay pot, beneath our red geranium.

I was four years older when my grandparents explained that during the war being associated with Jewish people, including close loving friends, could cost you your life. They also revealed that the package Mamie had brought home at great risk contained Mabel's jewelry. Among her treasures was a precious heirloom, Mabel's most cherished possession. Her father's gold signet ring etched with a Star of David.

My Mother's Fur Coat
February 1943

My mother and I began our afternoon together, standing side by side in front of Claussen's Toy Shop. Despite the cold February wind, I stared in silence, mesmerized by this week's new, cluttered, window display. "*Alors, mon trésor,* are you ready? *Oui? Alors,* let's go inside."

My heart beat faster when we entered the dusty, narrow shop with its familiar, faintly acrid scent emanating from Monsieur Claussen's remaining stock of pre-war, celluloid, rubber, and tin toys. Above us, the larger, bulkier toys were displayed, hanging from the tinned ceiling.

Every Saturday, on my mother's day off, we visited this shop where I was allowed to choose a trinket. Today, it was a green frog with bulging eyes. It would live with my collection of celluloid fish and boats, all stored until bath time in a round basket under the bathroom sink. Monsieur Claussen pulled out a deep drawer from which I selected my favorite, the one with the palest yellow belly. Grateful to escape

Maman and me on a winter's day.

from the confine of its dark wooden drawer, it smiled at me. "Oh, you'll be so happy to float in hot soapy water with your new friends," I whispered. Once wrapped, my frog was placed in my mother's purse for safekeeping and we left the shop.

"Ah, *mon trésor*, today we're going to visit my friend Arlette. You can look at all the pretty jewelry in the glass cases. We'll go to the park next week." How disappointing. We visited Arlette in her father's shop once before. I recalled its rancid, stale tobacco smell, the dimness caused by a drawn curtain, so heavy and thick, fresh air could never pass through to reach their living quarters in the back.

Leaving our tram behind at the busy Place de la Bourse, we made our way along awkward, narrow sidewalks, leading us deeper into this humble section of old Brussels. We followed ancient, dank smelling streets, where sunlight had long ago given up trying to reach down below to shed light upon these desolate, worn structures.

"*Oui, voila.* Here we are," my mother whispered, as she tapped on the glass panel of the door. From behind the curtain in the back, Arlette rushed out to unlock the bolt. The bell on the back of the door signaled our entrance. As we stepped inside, her father appeared, "*Eh, non! Non!* That's not a good idea. Why did you bring your daughter along?"

My mother blushed. "Oh, but, she will be fine. She can stay here in the shop. *Ah, oui,* she'll be fine." He shook his head and turned away, but she followed him behind the curtain.

Arlette pointed to a high wooden stool. "Stay here."
She lifted me. "*Oui*. Sit right there. Don't touch anything. *Sois
sage*, be good. We'll be right back, in a few minutes. That's all."
When she raised a corner of the curtain, heavy cigarette smoke
escaped from the back room, along with muffled sounds of
men's voices. In an instant, she too disappeared through the
folds of the dense cloth.

Left alone perched on the stool, I was curious, but too
scared to disobey and peek behind the curtain. The smell of
simmering turnip soup drifted into the shop. It was not my
favorite scent. After a few minutes of feeling bored, I wriggled
down from the stool and studied meager jewelry displays in
the two glass cases: thin, gold chains, pinned to a worn, blue
velvet board alongside a few, left over, round and oval silver
medals for Saint Mary and other saints. Hung upon a black
velvet board were small gold crosses. Placed there a long time
ago, they seemed lost and forgotten. Four watches lay on a
wood tray alongside black and brown leather coin purses.

My mother burst out from behind the curtain. "*Voila*,
voila. Let's go." She grabbed my hand, and rushed for the
door, followed by Arlette who quickly unlocked it. In an
instant, we were back on the cold, dismal, sidewalk.
Remaining inside, hidden behind the closing door, Arlette
waved a brief "*Au revoir*," then she bolted the door.

"But, Maman, why didn't Arlette invite me inside
with you?"

A yellow Brussels tram, typical of the ones that took us on our many day-trips and outings. Look closely to see a street-sweeper to the left of the tram.

An old, dark Brussels street.
Artist unknown.

"Can you perhaps walk faster?" She tightened her grip on my wrist. "*Oui, très bien.* Yes, very good. That's it. Now let's just head back to the tram stop."

We hurried along the deserted, back streets. "Mmm. Oh, well, *mon trésor,* it seems today was not a good day for a visit with Arlette after all. But, perhaps next time she'll join us at the park. Would you like that?"

We boarded the tram and found two seats side by side. I knew this route, there would be lots to see. But as more passengers boarded, they blocked my view. This would not be a fun ride! After my mother offered my seat to a lady with a cane, I tried sitting on her lap. "*Non, non.* Oh, please. Not today."

"But, please, Maman, why not?"

Before she could reply, standing passengers were thrown off balance, then stumbled and fell upon each other as the conductor shouted a warning in Flemish, and applied the brakes with full force. The falling passengers froze in startled disbelief as the grinding wheels screeched against the metal rails, producing a screaming wail.

People shrieked as two men elbowed through the crowded tram, and fought their way to the back door. They shoved it open and jumped to the pavement. It was too late. Armed German soldiers surrounded the tram. Caught at once, both men were punched then thrown to the ground. Dazed, arms bound, their faces bleeding, they were dragged away, stumbling.

Inside the tram, panic ruled. Orders shouted in German were heard from outside. Within moments, soldiers carrying rifles invaded the car. "*Alle hier bleiben!* Everybody stay here!"

Holding back ferocious German shepherds, they separated the women from the men, and with great efficiency, began searching each passenger. Near the front, a youth was grabbed from his mother's side, then shoved toward the group of men standing in the rear of the tram. Identity papers were checked. The women, some seated, whispered. Several began to cry. Strangers moments ago, they huddled closer together, a few crossing themselves, before frantically searching in their purses for their identification cards.

My mother gripped my hand. With her other trembling hand, she pressed her identification card against her.

"Don't say anything," she whispered in my ear.

"About what, Maman? Say anything about what?"

"Nothing. Nothing at all." Then she was silent. Only her brown eyes spoke to me, filled with a fright I had never seen before.

I glanced at those guns. What would they do to us? What had we done wrong? A soldier with a menacing German shepherd made his way from the front of the tram. The dog wore a muzzle of leather straps, but stopped in front of us, sniffed the hem of my mother's fur coat, and drooled. When it snarled, I saw its long fangs and smelled its breath. I tried to make myself smaller. The soldier snapped, *"Komm' her!"* The dog snarled again, but followed the soldier who yanked it to the rear of the tram. I thought of Jolie, Madame Gruber's Pekinese, who lived downstairs and how well-mannered she was, offering her right paw when she heard, *"Bonjour."* Poor Jolie wouldn't stand a chance if she met this German dog. I knew that just for fun, it would pick Jolie up, shake her, and then kill her. I shuddered.

Soldiers in the back, using their rifle butts, concentrated on selecting, then shoving the able-bodied men off the tram. One holding his gun by the barrel, swung it hard and cracked the back of a muscular workman. The skinny, awkward boy was ordered to follow the men.

Standing on my toes, I caught glimpses of them lined up outside, their hands held above their heads. I could not bear to see more, and buried my face into my mother's warm coat. For an instant I caught a trace of her perfume in the soft brown fur, its familiar, heady scent reassuring. If I didn't look anymore, perhaps all this would go away.

A young, blond German soldier grabbed my arm, yanked me aside and shoved me into the group of standing women. I screamed.

"I want *ma* Maman! I want *ma* Maman!"

The frightened women held me back. One tightened her grip on my shoulders so hard it hurt. She covered my head with her coarse wool shawl and clamped her hand over my mouth. Leaning down, she hissed in my ear, "I'm warning you *petite gosse*, little kid, be quiet. Just hush or you'll get us all in trouble with that screaming."

The smell from the thick shawl sickened me. It reeked of stale cooking grease and sour pipe tobacco. I couldn't breathe.

Another woman whispered, "*Oh, mais non! Non!*" As I gagged, she released her hand and the shawl was pulled away.

Standing by my mother, the young soldier motioned toward me.

"*Ist das deine kleine Tochter?*" Is that your little daughter? My mother spoke some Italian and German. She replied, "*Doch. Das ist meine Tocher.*" Yes, yes. That is my daughter.

"*Wie alt ist sie?*"

"Oh, but – She's only four."

He pointed his rifle and glared at me, signaling me to stay back. The women held me tighter. I watched as my mother raised her arms above her head. The soldier parted her fur coat and began to search her. Abruptly, he stopped. For a moment they stared at each other. He lowered his head and turned away.

He shouted. "*Macht schnell. Setz dich. Ja. Du! Schnell! Schnell!*" Make it fast. Sit down. Yes. You. Fast! Fast! He tapped my shoulder with his rifle and nodded for me to go back and sit next to my mother. He stepped away and began to search the next woman, the one who covered my head. Crying, I tried once more to hide under my mother's coat, but she pushed me aside to a seat on her left.

A green Nazi truck pulled up. German soldiers pointed their guns and shouted, "*Rauss! Rauss! Rauss!*" In single file, with their arms still raised above their heads, the able-bodied men and the boy were ordered to climb into the waiting truck. Two burly guards, their rifles ready, stood nearby.

The boy's mother screamed and broke away from the group of terrified women. She ran to a window and clawed at the glass. "Marcel! Marcel! *Oh, Mon Dieu!*" She sobbed. "*Non! Non!* He's my son!"

"Maman! Maman!" Marcel turned to see his mother through the tram window, but the guard swung his rifle and jabbed the boy's ribs. He stumbled, and his blue *béret* fell to the ground. With one hand still held above his head he reached down to retrieve it, but hesitated. The hefty guard laughed as his companion kicked the *béret* beneath the truck.

"*Das ist das ende von seinnem béret!*" That is the end of his *béret!* Then, he kicked Marcel while the other guard grabbed him. Together, they both shoved and pushed until Marcel disappeared into the truck.

The search of the remaining women completed, only one was taken away by the soldiers. Sobbing, she was driven away in a black car. The truck was already gone.

"Tell me, Maman, tell me, am I going to be taken away from you? Will they put me inside a truck, too? Is that what will happen? Please tell me?"

"*Oh, non. non, mon trésor.* We'll be going home

together, but please be quiet. You'll see. All this will be over soon. Now, close your eyes," she whispered. Tears fell from her cheeks to disappear into the dark fur of her coat.

His wrists untied, the conductor was shoved back on board the tram and ordered to resume driving. "*Mach, schnell. Fahr los.*" Move it fast. Move away.

The remaining passengers, some still crying, returned to their seats. In the back of the tram, Marcel's mother was comforted by two women trying to soothe her. When the tram resumed its route, and proceeded along the rails toward Rue Sainte Catherine, panic slowly subsided, replaced by murmuring comments. "She was so young." "Oh, my God. So young to be taken away like that," someone added. "*Eh oui,* and so pretty too."

Sitting across from us, a woman sneered. "*Hein, oui,* but some of us know just how to speak in German to the enemy." Louder so all could hear, she questioned, "*Eh,* why not? Maybe speaking German and being a beautiful lady provides special treatment?"

From the back an old man shouted. "*Ouhai, ouhai,* that's right. Maybe just like that fine fur coat!"

Her face flushed, my mother pulled the cord, grabbed my hand, and rushed us to the back door of the tram. "But, Maman, this isn't our stop. It's too soon to get off."

She shoved the door open. "Never mind, step down. Now!" With glaring, angry faces pressed against the windows, our tram rolled away, its wheels grating upon the metal tracks, leaving us behind on the cold sidewalk.

"Maman, I don't understand. We got off too soon. Why?" Passersby stared. Trembling, she adjusted my scarf.

"You see, *mon trésor*, those people turned against us. We had to get off. It wasn't safe on that tram anymore."

"But they are Belgians. Like us. Why?"

"Oh, they resented us. That's all."

During the cold walk back to my grandparent's apartment, I was tired and frightened. I knew now that no place was safe from the Nazis, and strangers could also be mean. I must remember all this. It would be difficult, but I had to try. I had to.

Riding in the elevator, I asked, "Tell me, please, what about the boy, Marcel? How will his Maman ever find him again?" But, my mother did not answer. Her hands held against her face, she turned away. Sobbing, she could not hear me.

Minutes later, we stood in our kitchen with my anxious grandparents. Then, just as Mamie confirmed Augustine had the day off, my mother laid her fur coat on the table. How strange. Pressing a cold compress to her forehead, she collapsed onto a chair and related details of our tram ride.

Tired and confused, I went to my room to play with my doll, Suzette. Moments later, I heard broken murmurs. "Ah, *la, la* . . . *chérie* . . . last time . . . *non* . . . dangerous . . . not . . . life . . . happened . . . both."

I returned to the kitchen and heard my mother

whisper. "*Mais oui*, look. *Voila, voila.*" In seconds, from the brown satin lining of her coat she retrieved a well-wrapped package tied with a string, and handed it to my grandmother. My grandfather removed the coat from the table, carried it to the salon and draped it over a chair. Our yellow and white checkered tablecloth now had a mound of fresh country butter as the centerpiece.

My grandmother removed a red meat fillet from the package and placed it on a platter. "Look, *mes enfants*, a real beefsteak! I'll prepare some potatoes *tout de suite*, right away. *Oui*, tonight is truly a feast!"

Holding Suzette, I ventured to the salon to inspect my mother's coat. Below her three embroidered gold initials, a section of stitches along the edge of the satin lining was undone. I reached inside, and slipped my hand right into a deep, secret, burlap pocket, sewn inside the shiny lining. Years later, I understood how brave she had been, and why, that day, on that infamous tram ride, she refused to allow me to sit on her lap.

"What is Marcel eating tonight for his supper?"

After a long silence, my grandmother turned away from the stove. "Oh, I'm certain it's sauerkraut and sausage. I understand it is the favorite dish in Germany."

My mother dabbed her eyes. "*Oui, oui*, that is true. And he'll have potatoes, too."

"But tell me, how long will those soldiers keep him away from his Maman?"

My grandfather seemed to ponder my question. "Oh, only two or three days, *ma chérie*, until they paint a little bridge, blue. *Ah, oui,* and after, the soldiers will bring him right back home, *ma petite*." Reassured, I helped set the silverware. That night, I tasted bread with thick, real butter. But I did not like the smell or the taste of red meat.

The next morning, a package was waiting for me on the breakfast table. After yesterday's frightening experience, I had forgotten all about my frog. Still sleepy, I opened the package, but my frog's fat belly had a gash and so did the top of its head.

"*Ah, non.* Well, it would seem your little frog was injured yesterday in your mother's purse by passengers shoving each other," explained my grandfather.

Together we placed it into a water filled bowl, but it refused to float and in moments, exuding small bubbles, it sank to the bottom. I cried, but my grandfather covered the bowl with one of his monogrammed handkerchiefs.

"*Oh, la, la,*" he whispered. "This poor frog needs to rest, but by tomorrow it will be tiptop. And now, shhh." That evening, we agreed to peek under the handkerchief. My frog was still resting at the bottom, unable to float.

"*Ah,* but, you must be patient, *ma petite*. These things take time. Tomorrow, your frog will be like new. I promise."

He was right. Before lunch the next day, he lifted the handkerchief, "*Et, voila*." My frog, floating in the bowl, was grinning at me. Its belly had turned a bit darker yellow, but I did not mind.

It took days before I left "our nest" without panic, or crying. With time the nightmares disappeared, but my fear of green Nazi trucks remained permanent. And, whenever we passed the corner, Rue du Marché aux Poulets, where the Nazis seized our tram, I still heard Marcel's voice and recalled the terror in his eyes as he turned and called out, "Maman! Maman!"

Monsieur Booth and *le Jazz*
April 1943

I had survived another long, boring, Sunday family dinner in our tenth-floor nest with my grandparents and my parents. Spring had arrived, the day was mild, and the April sunlight beckoned me to come outside. It was customary for European children in that era to be silent while at the table, and since my father was present, I was not allowed to speak during the meal. But after dessert, as Augustine served coffee, I asked, "to please be excused and play on the terrace?" They answered, "*Oui.*" As I gathered my two favorite dolls and the new book I had received for my birthday, my grandmother layered my body with a coat and a muffler. From the salon, my grandfather brought a cushion for me to sit on. Outside on our terrace, the air was fresh. At last, I was free.

I removed my coat, then, holding my dolls, I lay upon the cushion and stared up at the great white clouds slowly passing high above me, still listening to bits of their conversation. Cigarette smoke from the dining room

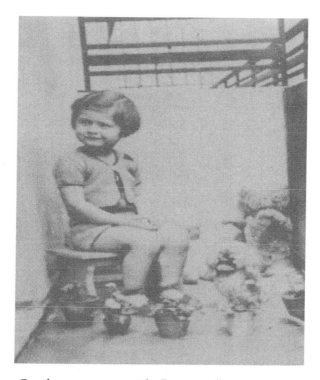

On the terrace outside "our nest" one summer day, with Teddy. I am looking toward Monsieur Booth's apartment.

drifted outside. In the salon, my grandfather turned on the radio for the Sunday afternoon concert. Soon, everyone finished their coffee and headed toward the salon to join him and relax. I heard the familiar clatter of dishes as Augustine cleared the table. I was *très contente*, very happy, and as I looked at pictures in my new book the sunlight on my face felt so warm and comforting, I dozed off.

Unfamiliar voices and laughter awakened me. Fascinated, I listened. Never had I heard so many voices, different conversations, all at the same time. How odd. I tiptoed to the end of the long, narrow terrace. Holding my breath, I crouched down so I could listen without being seen. After a few moments, I stood up when I realized that the cement wall separating both terraces was higher than the top of my head, while the wrought-iron partition would help me to remain unseen. Excitement ran through my body. I shivered. To see and not be seen. How perfect. I stood on my toes, took my first peek, and could not stop staring at a fantasy on the next balcony.

Flower-filled urns lined one side of the terrace, and all the glass doors were thrown open, allowing sunlight and springtime into the apartment. I was impressed. There was nothing like that in my world. These people greeted and celebrated spring, while our apartment, with its cocooned layers of gauzy curtains and plum velvet drapes, remained so solemn. Taking a second peek, I saw couples drifting in and out of the terrace. Everyone was happy. This was a revelation for me. I had never seen so many happy people at the same time. Everybody held a glass, while trays of *hors d'oeuvres* were passed around. Next door was far more to my liking than our formal surroundings.

To see better, I stood on the cushion. Now I could see couples dancing in the living room on a dark, polished parquet floor, under a crystal chandelier. They must have been very good friends, because some were kissing and holding each other tight. Flickering candles were everywhere. How strange. In "our nest" we lit small candles on our birthday cakes, larger red ones at Christmas and, sometimes, in church after mass on Sundays, we lit long white ones, but never so many as this.

As I wondered about so many lit candles on a sunny spring Sunday in one's apartment, the music caught my attention. It was strange, not too loud, but with a lot of odd notes. It seemed to make everyone happy. Someone shouted, "*Vive le jazz*," as another disk was played. I knew then that there was another world beside our own cloistered one. And one day I, too, would play jazz, and give parties where everyone danced and kissed and was happy together. Except at my parties, I would also invite beautiful ladies.

While I day-dreamed about wonderful parties in my future, my grandmother suddenly appeared. After a quick peek through the partition, she marched me off to the salon. Still in awe I babbled, "I think I like jazz. What a *superbe* apartment Monsieur Booth has. Why can't we have a party like that?"

Once in the salon, filled with the Sunday concert sounds of yet another Wagner opera, this due to the German control of Brussels' radio station, my grandmother whispered, "Ah, *petite chérie*, but you must *absolument* forget anything you saw next door this afternoon."

But, how could I?

From that day on, whenever Monsieur Booth rode in the elevator with us, I took great delight in admiring his elegant attire and enjoyed faint whiffs of his light-citrus cologne. Not very tall and extremely trim, he stood rigid, wearing tight-fitting, tailored tweed jackets in tones to compliment his sandy hair and pale English complexion. These were paired with perfectly pressed, charcoal or light grey, flannel wool trousers. His rich, leather loafers or plush, brown suede shoes were immaculate, and, on his arm, he often carried a black and beige, plaid umbrella, probably from England. I always gave him my best smile in silent gratitude for showing me a new exciting world which I knew, one day, I would visit and enjoy again. "*Vive le jazz.*"

That was the last spring Monsieur Booth was our next-door neighbor. Curious about his absence, I asked my grandparents. "Ah, *la, la*, but we've told you before. He's away. Now please stop asking."

But one day, my mother finally confided. "Ah, *oui, mon trésor, oui*. Monsieur Booth has left. You see, he went back to England to be with his *petite* Maman, *chérie*."

Still not convinced, a few days later, just to be sure, I

asked Juliette. Her face flushed. She looked away, then stammered, "Oh, he's gone on a trip. *Oui*, that's right, he's away. Shopping."

"But, where?"

"Oh, he's gone to Antwerp to buy a new suitcase." This puzzled me even more. Couldn't Monsieur Booth have found a new suitcase here in Brussels without traveling all the way to Antwerp? He must have wanted quite a fine suitcase.

For a long time after, whenever I played on the terrace, I peeked through the wrought-iron partition, but nothing ever stirred. A corner chair, shoved against the window, had left one of the sheer drapery panels slightly parted. Perfectly still, forlorn, the chair waited, as I did. Waited for his return. Waited for his next party with his friends and the sounds of jazz.

Years later, I learned the truth. One night, while I slept, my elegant Monsieur Booth was dragged away from his apartment next door by the Gestapo.

He never returned.

The Blue Letter
May 1943

On Thursdays, *le facteur*, delivered the mail late. Since our mailbox was at the bottom row within easy reach, I was allowed to open it, retrieve the mail and hand it to my grandfather. Once he glanced through it, he would take my hand, "*Merci bien*. And now *petite*, let us return upstairs. Mamie is waiting for us. Supper is almost ready."

This evening, when I opened the metal box, something familiar was inside. One of those blue letters, from my great-grandmother in Brittany. Its pretty, colorful French stamps covered over by heavy, black German markings.

"*Ce soir*, your Mamie will be happy when you hand her this blue letter, ma petite."

He was right. Once we returned upstairs, my grandmother did smile. "*Merci ma chérie*. But, supper is ready. Let us sit down while it's hot. We'll read Mémé's letter afterwards."

Later, in the salon, my grand-père settled in

his leather club-chair, I lay on the oriental rug with Teddy, my head propped up by one of the plum velvet pillows. And once my grandmother sat, snuggled into the corner of the plum settee, she opened the blue letter and began to read.

Samedi, le 15 mai, 1943

Mes chers enfants,

First of all, let me reassure you. Everything is well now. Everything is back to normal and I am still here, safe in our house, just as before. However, I must tell you of the frightening last two days.

German troops have recently increased their presence here. More and more they are seen patrolling along our roads. Thursday, around two o'clock, four German soldiers entered the garden. They spoke while walking around to the back of the house. *Naturellement*, I could not understand a word, since it was German. After passing through our stone larder into the rear courtyard, they came back, banged on the front door, furiously yanking the bell at the same time. *Evidemment* I had to let them in. Oh, *mes enfants,* what would your *cher* Papa have said? Me, now his widow, allowing Germans entry into his house! *Mais,* can you possibly imagine such a thing?

The officer in charge signaled his three men to remain in the hall. He led me into the dining room then saw how frightened I was. Speaking some French in a heavy German accent, he assured me no harm would come to me, but stated they were here to sequester the house! He asked for the number of rooms and bathrooms and ordered his men to search upstairs.

I won't soon forget the dread I felt hearing German boots on our stairs. In shock, I could not even speak. He pointed to a chair, and told me to sit. He noticed I was dressed in mourning and asked, "*Vous êtes une veuve*, Madame?"

I answered him, "*Oui*. I am a widow. My husband died five months ago."

"A very large house for an older woman alone. *N'est ce pas*, Madame? Isn't it?" He sneered. "And so, where are your children then?"

Ah, mes chéris, I will never forget what happened next. Before I could reply, he stepped closer to study Papa Arthur's medals hung all along the wall — his framed *Légion d'Honnheur*, his British Distinguished Service Order signed by King George V, his Belgian appointment by King Albert as an Officer of the Crown, and *naturellement*, many others. In silence he stared at Papa Arthur's military photograph for several seconds.

"Your husband apparently was a great Commander, Madame. He did his duty as a French Army officer. I see he fought well for his country during our previous war." He paused to clear his throat. "Therefore, Madame, as a

German officer, in this case I cannot and will not allow his house to be taken from his widow and children."

After he saluted Papa Arthur's photograph, he clicked his heels. "*Mes condoléances*, Madame. *Bonsoir*," and walked out. From the hall, he called upstairs to his men. A moment later their car was gone.

Bouleversée, shaking, I secured the lock on the front door, went to bed and prayed. I fell asleep later, while saying my rosary.

As I told you, we are seeing more German troops. They have brought in forced labor to build more fortifications along our coasts. Walking to the outdoor market yesterday, I saw columns of men, poorly dressed, marching along the cliffs toward the Port of Dahouët. And now, *en plus de ça*, on top of this, there is nightly activity at the end of our own street! With Monsieur Gérard gone, his widow has turned his modest Café du Coin into a thriving business. *Oui, mes enfants!* His *veuve* now entertains German officers with ample alcohol, fine French food, loud music and some believe, a few willing farm girls from nearby villages. *Dieu Merci*, thank God, Papa Arthur is no longer here to witness such *ordure*, garbage, down the road from his own house!

And now, I end this letter as I must also inform Yvonne in Rome, but apparently, even if my letters even reach her, they are censored. Most words remaining are impossible for her to reconstruct.

The kind Madame Jouvel has promised to stop by tomorrow with a few eggs and green beans from her garden. I will write to you again, next week.

Je termine this letter with tender thoughts to *la petite*, to Simone and to you both,

Votre,
Mémé

By the time, my grandmother finished reading the letter she was in tears, and I did not understand why. But, something bad had happened. Something in Mémé's house. Far away. German soldiers went in her garden. They saw something on the walls. Why didn't Mémé like the music? Nothing made sense. My grandfather stood at her side, comforting her.

"Why are you crying Mamie?"

She dabbed her eyes then whispered, "*Non, non. Tout va bien, petite.* All is well."

Clutching the blue letter, my grandfather repeated, "*Un miracle*, Alice. *Oui, franchement,* truly *un miracle.*"

Twenty years later, while visiting with my grandparents, now living in the house in Brittany, I was shown Mémé's letter. When I read it aloud, the words on the now fragile blue paper still brought us tears. Tears of gratitude for the German officer who proved, on that day, to be a man of honor.

Le Monsieur Nègre
June 1943

Once a month, nineteen-year-old Juliette, our new live-in nanny, visited her family in the countryside for the day. My grandmother believed in the benefits of "fresh air and sunshine," so I was sent along. I enjoyed going to the farm, watching the cows being milked, chasing a certain rooster in the barnyard, and eating buttered country bread her mother sliced from gigantic, dark, round loaves. During our long tram ride back to Brussels, often carrying a jar of red jam and freshly cut flowers, I'd nestle my face in the bouquet, reminiscing about our day. But, just before we reached our stop, Juliette opened her blue compact to show me my nose, smudged by orange pollen. We'd always giggle as she wiped it away with her handkerchief.

These country journeys began with our walk along the shop-lined Rue de Flandre. Once we reached the canal near Quai des Charbonnages, we followed its bordering path while slow-moving supply barges, a red Nazi flag flying at the stern,

Our Juliette and me at her family's farm.

passed by. Sometimes, two or three German guards stood on board, holding rifles. After a ten-minute walk, we arrived at the solitary tramway terminus. Its shabby, green walls with peeling fragments of faded old movie posters were now plastered with German placards listing the latest, strict Nazi ordinances.

The first time we came to the terminus, I had asked Juliette about the torn colored posters.

"Oh, those? They are from old movies." Her voice trailed away. "Ah, *oui*. But all that was before the war."

"But tell me please," I had asked, trying not to look at the scary Nazi eagle, "what does it say on all those grey papers with that mean looking bird at the top?"

Juliette grabbed my hand and pulled me away. "Ah, *non! Non!* We don't look at those."

"But why?"

"Those are German ordinances. With all their warnings of punishments. Imagine! Telling us what to do in our own country! Those *sales Boches!* Come away from there. *Oui.* Let's go stand over here, *petite.*"

Seized with fear, I wondered, could we perhaps be punished for boarding a particular trolley? Was our day in the country even allowed? I tried to hide behind her, then glanced around for German soldiers lurking on the platform, waiting to take us away. Moments later, still fearful–when I asked Juliette about all this, she looked startled and shook her head.

"Oh, *non*, of course not. That's silly. Don't be afraid,

petite." She smiled. "*Oui, oui,* we'll be just fine. *Et voila,* look. Here comes our tram. Are you ready?"

It was at this terminus that several tramway lines ended. After a brief rest, the sluggish trolleys circled around the bend, and like giant, obedient beasts, each headed back toward its own separate destination.

But today, when we reached the terminus, the waiting riders did not stand under the shelter, but formed a semi-circle around something, or someone. Since our number twenty-eight tram was nowhere in sight, I begged Juliette to see what it was, and pulled her hand so she would walk faster. As we got closer, we heard musical sounds. It wasn't a song, but bells and cymbals jingling and clanging. Several rows of people stood still, watching.

I let go of her hand, ran and wriggled my way to the front of the crowd, knowing she would find me. Once in the front row, I became spellbound by a man dressed in a beautiful, short, tight, plaid jacket, green trousers and a derby hat. A rectangular blue tray hung from his neck by a leather strap. There, packed in tight rows, were tins of licorice, mints, fruit pastilles, as well as an assortment of bonbons and nuts packed in small, cellophane bags. I had never seen such a variety of candy! Slowly prancing through the crowd, he displayed this cache of delights for all to see, then hopefully, buy. He held a long red leash, and at the end was a small monkey wearing a red jacket with brass buttons and a flat red hat held by a strap under its chin. The monkey climbed a tower of crates, and when told to do so, shook the string of bells and hit the cymbals to produce loud, rhythmic sounds.

Now by my side, Juliette held my hand as we enjoyed the performance and found the monkey's grimaces amusing. The nattily dressed man passed in front of us with his overflowing tray, and soon people began exchanging francs for their selected treats. This pleased the monkey, and perched high above the crowd he doubled up on his antics. I noticed a button was missing from the man's slightly frayed plaid jacket. His leather shoes appeared worn and dusty.

Juliette refused to purchase a bag of bonbons. "*Oh, non. Non,* your grandmother would never approve. It isn't sanitary." But I did not care. I was captivated by the monkey and curious about the candy vendor, for I had never seen a black person.

"Juliette, tell me please, why does he paint his face and hands black? Is it done every morning after he takes his bath?"

"*C'est un* Monsieur *Nègre,*" Juliette replied. He is a Negro gentleman. "He comes from the Congo, another country very far away, where the sun is always hot, and there are tall palm trees and tigers everywhere."

Her explanation intrigued me even more. When we boarded our tram, I ran to the rear and got a window seat all the way in the back, so I could still see him. With everyone aboard, the tram pulled away. I felt sad and cried a little.

If he was from the Congo, why was he here? So far away from home selling bags of bonbons on this bleak corner of the tramway terminus in Brussels, with his little monkey at his side? Why did he run away from his Maman and his beautiful palm trees? He must be homesick and lonely here in Brussels. How would he get back home to his tigers? Perhaps one of the barges on the canal might know the way.

As a misty rain began to fall, I decided tonight I would definitely mention all of this to my grandfather. He would sort it out for me.

The Aviator
July 1943

Except for my new sandals, which gave me blisters, it was a perfect day in July. Fortunately, Juliette had some adhesive bandages in her satchel, which she applied to my feet as we rode the yellow tram. I loved sitting next to her by the window, looking at passing new sights. Corner street carts offered fresh mackerel, mussels and smoked herring to hurried shoppers, while the vendors' dogs lay sleeping beneath the carts. Our tram continued passed open air markets, where people bought whatever little food was available, passed kiosks surrounded by customers waiting their turn, as others walked away savoring hot, salty *pommes frites*, French fries, nestled in newspaper cones. We passed churches set back from the street. Small squares with monuments in the center, and benches where people enjoying the summer sun sat talking or reading their newspapers. Today we were headed into the Belgian countryside on an important errand: to purchase fresh honey, my grandfather's favorite treat, which he enjoyed on his

Juliette called me, "The Countryside Princess
of all the Wheat Fields."

morning toast and reluctantly shared. We would also bring back peaches from the farmer himself, and fresh eggs, unavailable in Brussels.

My grandmother and I discovered this farm during one of our country outings for "fresh air and sunshine." This morning, she handed Juliette a piece of paper.

"Juliette, here is the list and directions to the farm. Please make sure you bring back the most important item, fresh honey for Monsieur. He has just finished the last jar."

Juliette glanced at the list, "Ah, *oui, oui*, Madame, but of course." She turned to me, "Now hurry up. Go, *vite, vite*. We'll miss our tram."

She slipped the folded paper in her sweater pocket as we exited the apartment, ready for our day's adventure. But, just as our tram pulled away, she was unable to find the paper. Her eyes filled with tears.

"*Non, non*, Juliette, don't worry," I assured her. "I remember the way."

After a ten-minute walk, we stood at the stone entrance to the farm. Juliette, speaking in Flemish, managed to get us the honey, peaches, fresh eggs and best of all, a thick slab of smoked bacon — a rare treat. This sent her into a detailed description of her country soup recipe, which she would prepare for us tomorrow.

"Naturally, I'll be careful and use only a portion of this precious bacon, but it's the key ingredient in creating my delicious soup."

Pleased with the success of our country expedition, except for the problem of my sandals, we headed back. Walking along, we sang fragments of a new song by Edith Piaf. I didn't understand the words, but Juliette taught me the refrain, and we laughed as I sang the words "*Je trouve ça merveilleux*" I find that marvelous — with her over and over. Along the way, I picked red poppies and daisies growing by the country road. We sat at the edge of a wheat field, and after replacing the bandages, Juliette made a crown with the flowers.

Using a deep voice, she declared, "With this wreath I appoint you Countryside Princess of all the Wheat Fields," and she placed it on my head, securing it using my hair barrettes, while I clapped my hands and giggled.

It was then we heard a strange, sputtering noise from above, like a motor. We looked up, and saw a black smoky line in the sky. The line slowly began forming a graceful black arc heading down toward the ground, not far from where we sat. With wonder, I noticed something else in the sky — a strange bird — but it was not flying, it was floating toward the earth. A look of panic appeared on Juliette's face. She crossed herself and held me against her as we stood, in order to see more. She cried out,

"Ah, *Mon Dieu*, it's an aviator! Oh, thank God, he's alive." Holding my hand, her voice shaky, she explained how his white silk parachute had just saved him.

There was a small, red brick farmhouse on the left,

across the way from where we stood. The farmer, his wife holding a baby, and the grandmother were cautiously coming out of their house. Just as they stepped onto the country road to have a closer look, Germans on motorcycles roared by, coming out of nowhere, and heading toward the black smoke at the far end of the wheat field.

"Let's walk across the road," Juliette suggested. "We'll see much better." She hurried me along. After we gathered our valuable provisions, we joined the farmer and his family. They spoke in Flemish. I did not understand a word, but the farmer explained to Juliette that it was a single engine American fighter plane, since the Americans flew their missions in the daytime, while the British bombed only at night.

We waited a few minutes, then heard the motorcycles returning. This time they were not roaring, they were going slow, very slow. Several men in uniform followed, walking three abreast on the narrow, curved road, four yards away from us, their rifles drawn, ready to shoot. They wore the olive green Nazi uniforms, except for one. Surrounded by the German soldiers, he walked as best he could, limping and wincing from pain.

As he got closer, I noticed that his beige trousers were torn at the knee and he wore a brown leather jacket. Tall, he had wavy blond hair. His skin was ruddy. A thin line of blood trickled down his left cheek, but as his hands were held above his head as a sign of surrender, he could not wipe his face and the long, white, silk scarf around his neck was spotted red. He was their prisoner.

Juliette leaned down to whisper, "Be quiet. Don't move." She gripped my shoulders. "*Ah, Mon Dieu, ma petite. Oh! Mon Dieu.* Oh, please do not say a word."

At that moment, the handsome American prisoner passed in front of us. He was the aviator shot down by the Germans. That was his airplane burning. He was the parachutist we had seen floating back to earth minutes ago.

I looked into his eyes for an instant. A brief moment. I wanted to. I wanted him to know how sorry we were for his crash, and now his capture. Surprised to see us standing there, he smiled, and then — he winked at me. A trail of cords, still attached to his parachute straps, made a soft, steady, rhythmic sound as they bounced along on the dusty country road, following him obediently, like a well-trained dog, as he bravely limped away from us.

Juliette spoke a few words to the farmer and his family who sadly headed back inside their farm house. In silence, we walked back toward the tramway stop with our provisions, but they seemed heavier and more difficult for us to carry than before. I was still wearing my crown, but the magic of it had disappeared.

That night we repeated our story several times to my mother and grandparents. After supper, my grandfather opened his new jar of honey and offered me a large spoonful, "To help sweeten your dreams, *ma petite chérie.*"

Later, before I went to bed, Juliette and I knelt

and prayed together for the dashing, tall and brave American fighter pilot who had fallen from the sky that afternoon.

Nazis On a Summer Afternoon
August 1943

Our footsteps echoed on the bare parquet floors as I glanced at our fleeting, fragmented, reflections in the mirrored panels of the corridor. My mother held my hand as she led me to the far end of the penthouse. We entered the blue room, where the August afternoon sunlight filtered through gauze panels on the doors to the balcony. This was my paternal grandmother's boudoir, lined with built-in, mirrored armoires, her blue velvet daybed with plump cushions facing the balcony. Next to a double, white porcelain sink was the door to the pristine, white tiled bathroom with its giant tub. A square table with an embroidered linen cloth was centered in the room, covered by an assortment of interesting bottles, jars, and containers. It was immaculate.

Today was Saturday and my parents and I were having the usual formal dinner and visit at my paternal grandparents' home where "Children should be seen and not heard." My mother propped some velvet pillows on the daybed and helped

Nazis paraded every chance they could. Here they
are in front of the Royal Palace, four blocks
from the apartment of my paternal grandparents.
On the day I sneaked a look from their kitchen
terrace, as the parade passed by, it created a great
disturbance within the family. By unspoken agreement,
Belgians did not watch these parades.

me climb up. She unfolded a shawl and placed it over me. "*Ah, voila*, look at your new book. Soon you'll be sleepy and enjoy a nice nap. I'll be back. *Sois bien sage*, be very good." She kissed me, turned away and closed the door. I listened to the fading sounds of her footsteps until she reached the end of the corridor and re-joined the grown-ups in the salon.

I glanced through my picture book, but I was bored. I climbed down to inspect my grandmother's dressing table, and with no one around, I did the forbidden thing and touched her jars of creams, the different shaped glass bottles of lotions, rose water, the perfume bottle with its flower glass stopper, the powder box with its funny tumbling puffs on its black and orange lid. I couldn't resist lifting the satin bow on the puff made from blue cygnet feathers. It tickled when I touched it to the tip of my nose. To decide which one smelled the best I opened all the jars. My favorite was an apricot-colored one. The cream inside even smelled like apricots. But I became confused as to which top went to what jar, and as I tried different combinations – I saw them.

There on my grandmother's dressing table was a pair of black binoculars. These were larger and bulkier than the ones my other grandfather had at home, and since I had been allowed to look through his, I was sure it would be all right to look through these, if I was careful. But even with the leather strap around my neck they were heavy to lift and when I looked through them everything in the room was blurred.

I moved toward the balcony. Perhaps I could see

clouds. I slid behind the sheer curtains, stepped out to the narrow terrace, braced the binoculars against my face and looked up.

Blue. More blue. Blue sky. Oh, clouds, beautiful, soft, white clouds. I moved the binoculars. Something red. It stirred. My eyes travelled up. More red. A Nazi flag on a roof top.

Ah, oui! The *Kommandantur.* Two streets over. Its flag fluttering in the warm, gentle breeze.

To the bottom left something moved. A Nazi officer. Coming out on the roof in his black boots, jodhpur pants and a white tank undershirt. He wore his officer's visor cap and carried things under his arms and in both hands. What was it? He walked a few steps, leaned down, down some more and — *oh, Mon Dieu!* I gasped. *Oui!* Oh, *oui*, there were, I counted again, eight Nazis on the rooftop — in athletic shorts! Blankets and cushions had been placed on the flat roof while they sunbathed together with blonde German ladies in scanty, romp suits. But, some of these Nazi ladies had forgotten their tops! The officer threw his head back, laughed, and popped a cork from a bottle of champagne. He served two couples, then reached for another bottle and opened that one, too. They must have really liked the champagne. They kept making toasts, raising their glasses. Laughing.

I observed the rooftop high above Brussels, spellbound by bare-chested Nazis, their bodies glistening as they applied sun-oil to one another. This group of fit goldenlimbed Germans officers who, for now, did not care about the war, had seized this summer afternoon to worship the sun. Their sun-kissed bodies exuded an unfamiliar, healthy glow, while on this same afternoon, on the streets below, people were pale and morose. Their grey lives filled with fear, they did not think about or dare to sunbathe.

Nazis were different. I was mesmerized by their dazzling power. I slowly understood why they could laugh, sunbathe, and drink champagne. They were superior, and they owned us. Nazis surrounded us everywhere. Stunned by this revelation, I backed away from the terrace.

The door opened. I froze.

It was my grandfather.

"Oh, now you've done it!" Too late. I was caught, the leather straps still around my neck. He pointed his finger at me, and yanked the binoculars away so hard my neck hurt.

"If those Nazis on that rooftop caught you staring at them from this balcony, they'd send the Gestapo right over to our door. To this very apartment! We'd all be arrested. Beaten, then hauled away. You'd have been taken from your Maman. Is that what you want?"

I began to cry.

My mother appeared in the doorway. "Oh, but, what's wrong?"

"Simone! Please! Come and get your child!"

He then noticed the dressing table. I hadn't even tried to replace the tops on the jars. What a mess! After I was reprimanded by my mother, a grim silence filled the boudoir as everyone gathered around my grandmother's dressing table to restore its previous order and perfection.

This put an immediate end to our Saturday visit and within half an hour we murmured our rapid, "*Au revoirs.*" My grandmother refused to kiss me good-bye. My grandfather shook his head and muttered to my father, "Your daughter is *une enfant difficile,*" not an easy child, and turned away.

While we waited for the tram on Avenue Marnix, my mother wondered, "But, that's odd. What were those binoculars doing on the dressing table in the first place?"

My father shrugged and replied with a sarcastic smile. "Oh, my father enjoys watching the sometimes-colorful activities on the rooftop of the *Kommandantur.* This morning he simply forgot the binoculars were still there."

Neighbors
October 1943

A persistent ringing of the telephone woke us from our deep, comfortable sleep.

It was my mother.

"Oh, Papa! *Mon Dieu! Vous devez nous aider!*" You must help us! she said, crying to my grandfather. "It's the neighbors! It's them! They have done this! Jean has just been arrested by the Gestapo! *Oui, mais oui!* They broke the door down and now he's been taken away!"

For the past year, my father enjoyed taunting the new next-door neighbors, a couple from Breda, a town across the Holland border. Because they were not Belgians, he offended them during elevator rides with his silent attitude. Worse, he sometimes rushed into the elevator, closed the grilled door, then quickly pushed the down button. Whistling, he descended alone to the lobby, leaving his dumbfounded neighbors behind on the landing. Tonight, they seized the opportunity for their sinister revenge.

My father was listening to the British Broadcasting Company on his new, prized, short-wave radio. To help ground the antenna, he placed the radio set next to the fireplace wall of the salon. The neighbors, who heard everything on the other side of the wall, called the German authorities, for it was against the law to own such a radio, and to listen to the BBC. Since the closest *Kommandantur* was by Square Marché aux Grains, one street over, two men from the feared Gestapo arrived at once.

They assaulted my father, knocking over and breaking the glass-topped table and my mother's favorite, her blue crystal vase. They seized his radio, and before taking him away in handcuffs, declared, "You are hereby notified, the punishment for owning a short-wave radio is internment. Heil, Hitler!"

Once they left, dragging my father between them, my petrified mother, who had been watching in silence, called us and her in-laws for help. My family was aware of the neighborhood rumor that every morning at six a truck came to take the latest prisoners to their merciless, and often final, destinations.

Soon, my paternal grandfather, Edmond, arrived. After paying a hefty sum, he was successful in hiring a taxi driver willing to drive him across Brussels, a rare thing this time of night. Sitting in the salon, my grandfathers were grim with apprehension. Their heads together, they spoke urgently in low voices. They needed to act immediately. Time was short.

My grandmother spoke on the telephone, reassuring my mother, then my paternal grandmother. She tried to calm them both. While Juliette, half-awake, was busy in the kitchen making coffee, I slid out of bed, and holding my teddy bear, tip-toed to the salon. I climbed on the plum settee in the far corner, behind my two grandfathers' chairs, and covered my bare feet with the velvet pillows to keep them warm. Hugging Teddy for comfort, I listened to their intense, hushed conversation. I did not understand their words, but it sounded *très grave*.

I was too young to know war could turn neighbor against neighbor, that betrayal was common in the face of fear and survival. I did not know an elevator ride could be risky. That informers could be anywhere, even in our own building.

But that night, for the very first time, I sensed a menacing danger had silently crept into "our nest". Growing stronger, it was now slowly invading. Yet I also believed that my grandfathers, who both knew a lot, could fix it. Make it go away before it destroyed us.

In hushed voices, they made telephone calls. Then, leaving their coffees behind, and armed with only flashlights, they braved the curfew to walk in the middle of the night to the feared *Kommandantur*, five blocks away.

I would have been content to spend the rest of the night on the settee snuggled under those warm velvet pillows, but Juliette found me.

"Ah, *Mon Dieu*, *ah voila*, there you are! I've been

looking for you everywhere. *Oui. Alors*, let's go to bed now. *Mais oui.* It's the middle of the night. And don't forget Teddy."

Hand in hand, we walked down the hallway and passed Mamie, who was again on the telephone. But now she was crying. Once in my room, Juliette tucked me back in bed.

"Please, tell me Juliette, do you think everything is going to be all right?"

She leaned over, turned out the light, and whispered, "Oh, *oui, ma petite*, don't worry. *Oui*, close your eyes now. *Bonsoir, petite.*"

I drifted to sleep hearing fragments of my grandmother's voice still attempting to soothe my mother, and I wondered if, after all, Juliette really knew the truth.

The Gestapo kept my father for nearly two days. My mother confided, years later, he was miraculously released due to my paternal grandfather's acquaintance with the former Mayor of Brussels. He had been his physician for a number of years.

On the evening of his release, my parents came to have supper with us. Ill at ease, my father refused to discuss his experience. He winced from time to time. There were cuts on his hands and a dark bruise below his left eye. From time to time I glanced across the table, but did not stare for I knew he would get angry.

Much to my grandmother's disappointment, my parents left before dessert was served. It was her special semolina pudding, prepared that afternoon in honor of my father's safe return.

The neighbors' reaction on seeing him again must have been one of both shock and disappointment. Not only was he still alive, but he remained their next-door neighbor. They never spoke or rode in the elevator together again. Ever.

Fondants Défendu
November 1943

Returning home from Sainte Catherine's outdoor market on a blustery, November day, Juliette and I were surprised to find someone had left the heavy, forged-iron and glass door to our building, propped wide-open.

We entered the lobby. Juliette grabbed my hand and we both ran. "Ah, *la, la,* what luck! Hurry up, *vite, vite,* there's the elevator."

Just as the grill door was closing, we stepped into the empty elevator. Out of breath, we giggled with relief, but before Juliette pushed the tenth-floor button, our wood elevator slowly began its ascent, with its steadfast, familiar, grinding sound. We were still laughing, when the elevator stopped at the fifth floor and two Nazi officers got on while continuing their intense conversation in German.

Juliette cringed and stepped back into the corner from where she tried, unsuccessfully, to grab my hand. The elevator began its sluggish return to the lobby. It was at that moment,

I noticed that the familiar red light next to our number ten was not lit. I felt trapped. Suddenly, the space became very tight. The officers' ominous, domineering presence filled the elevator. Afraid at first, I looked down.

They wore high, black leather boots with a superb shine. I had never seen such boots; they seemed so powerful. Intrigued, I moved closer and looked up. Their uniforms were immaculate, but their fearsome presence was different, far more imposing than other German soldiers. Both were tall with long, grey overcoats, draped over their shoulders. Their well creased pants were tucked inside the high boots. They wore fancy military hats with the Nazi emblem above the black, glossy visor.

Again, I inched closer as I stared at one officer in particular. He had jet black hair. An odd, shiny black cross hung below the medals covering his chest. He stopped talking to his companion, and looked down.

"*Das ist ein schönes Kind,*" That is a beautiful child. He patted the top of my head with his large, gloved hand. I wasn't scared, because for an instant, when he touched me, I saw a touch of sadness in his powerful, dark eyes. He reached into the deep, left-side pocket of his military jacket and pulled out pale, colored candies called *fondants* and offered them to Juliette, signaling they were for me.

At once her face flushed and her body trembled. She turned away. Shaking her head, she refused in a firm, polite whisper, "Oh, *non. Non. Merci,* Monsieur, *mais non.*"

The elevator reached the lobby, but before the grill door opened, his black leather gloved hands gripped Juliette's wrists then forced open her clutched hands. "*Hier!*" he said, firmly placing the *fondants* in her trembling palms. Both Nazi officers exited, rushed past two German armed guards flanking our lobby's wide-opened front door. They disappeared into a waiting, long black limousine with red Nazi flags on both sides of the windshield.

Distraught, Juliette leaned against the elevator wall. Her auburn hair now disheveled, her face still red. This time, she pushed the button and the red light went on by our number ten. During the ride upstairs, I gathered three apples rolling on the brown mat. In her fear, Juliette had dropped our grocery bag.

Back in the safety of our kitchen, while my grand-mère sorted our purchases, Juliette placed the five, beautiful and intriguing German *fondants* on the table so I could see them up close. Two were pale pink, one was a soft green, and two were creamy white. They had lovely shapes, with ridges and curves, each topped with a silver or purple sugar bead.

I sat at the table admiring them, when my grandmother turned and with a firm voice said, "These should be disposed of at once." She paused, then added in a whisper, "But very discreetly, of course."

Tearing a piece of newspaper, she wrapped "*ces fondants Nazis*", stepped outside to the kitchen terrace and lifted the cast iron lid of the garbage chute. For an instant, I heard the bundle as it vanished down the dark, narrow tunnel of our tenth floor *poubelle*. This was followed by the grim thud of the lid.

Left numb by this final confirming sound, I stared at the table where, a moment ago, those captivating German *fondants* had been lined up before me. I was still admiring them, mentally. I had already chosen a pink one, as a starter. But in seconds they were banished, and now gone forever.

My grandmother lectured Juliette on the danger of accepting anything from the enemy, "It is simply *défendu*, forbidden." I was warned of the dangers of germs in the German officer's pocket. "Ah, *ma* my *pauvre petite*, who knows what else could have been in there? Do you realize those Nazi *fondants* were not even wrapped? *Ah, la, la . . . oh, Mon Dieu!*"

But, far more dangerous than germs in the candy, was a grim reality. The occupying Nazis could, at their will, take away a pretty girl like the one on the tram, or sequester apartments. In that case you were simply evicted with your belongings. Since our large, sunny, top floor apartment was quite desirable, my grandparents and my mother decided that, for a while, we would keep a low profile. For weeks after that episode, I was not allowed out with Juliette, and she was told to ride the elevator only to the sixth floor, run down the rest of the way, then exit our building by the back entrance. "Just to be safe, of course."

But why these two high-ranking officers were in our building remains a mystery.

En tout cas, in any case, I had been so close to the pretty Nazi *fondants*, I often thought of how they might have tasted. And I never forgot the sadness in the German officer's dark eyes as he patted my head.

After the war, I made certain to acquire my own *fondants*. From time to time on the way to school with my friend Marie-Anne, we'd stop at the elegant Confiserie Latour, off Boulevard Anspach, my favorite sweet-shop. We admired its rows of glass candy-urns, its pink and white fluted columns and rose marble floor.

It took us weeks sometimes to save enough francs to enter this fancy *confiserie*, where we savored the intoxicating aroma of rich, dark, Belgian chocolate, while making our selections. My preferred choice of *fondants* was the pale yellow one with its discreet lemon flavor, topped by a tiny, green, sugar leaf.

Yet, as Marie-Anne and I walked to school, nibbling our *fondants*, I still wondered if these were as good as those Nazi *fondants défendu* might have been.

A Gunshot
January 1944

The day began on a happy note of anticipation. After a morning spent on extra grooming, my braids tightly woven and wearing my Sunday, maroon plaid, taffeta dress, my grandmother and I left right after lunch for an afternoon tea with her friend, Marie-Thérese. I held my doll, and we boarded the tram at Place de Brouckère.

The ride was quite a distance, but interesting, since I got a window seat only two rows away from my grand-mère.

Leaving Place Rogier and the bustling city center, we passed through various neighborhoods, each very different, until the tram veered right unto a new street. Endless, this street ran in a straight line, like an arrow, across the city until reaching the tram terminus where it abruptly ended. This long, monotonous street was lined with identical, sad, narrow, brick row-houses, each with similar lace curtains hung in their single ground-floor windows. Even the chosen colors for their doors were cheerless: dark green, brown and, on some, an

"Our nest" at Rue Marché aux Porcs 12. We were on the top floor next door to Monsieur Booth, who lived at the corner on the far left.

awful red that clashed with the sienna bricks.

Years later, I came across the essence of this street in certain of Magritte's paintings, in which the Belgian painter captures that same uneasy sense of wonder. Does anyone live behind those brick facades, or are they merely stage-props?

From time to time, the tram slowed as we passed areas where recent bombs eliminated street corners. Symbols of wartime destruction, only jagged walls of apartment houses remained: wall portions with odd geometric markings of vanished staircases ascending to nowhere; fragmented sections of a yellow tile wall of what had been a small kitchen; the blue flowered wallpaper that, until a few days ago, made a pretty bedroom, now peeling away, its long uneven, torn fragments blowing in the cold January air. It seemed almost indecent to look. Remnants of people's private lives exposed for tram riders to stare upon day after day. At first, I wanted to turn away, but I couldn't. Slowly transfixed, I now yearned to see more and gaze upon this eerie scene of total devastation. In the distance, two women, carrying infants and grocery satchels, made their way around the still, smoldering piles of rubble, to reach the streets beyond.

Our tram continued until the street ended at a small, round-about park, above which loomed four or five trees. This was the terminus.

Continuing on foot, we passed older, imposing, town houses built of beige Belgian stone, boasting ornamental grill-work and massive, polished oak doors, reflecting Belgian middle-class affluence at the beginning of the century. Turning onto a side street, we stood in front of Marie-Thérèse's town house. Grateful it was spared in Tuesday's bombardment, which decimated houses only two blocks away, we rang the doorbell.

The vestibule was dark, but beyond it, a series of three rooms with windows at both ends, allowed sunlight to enter. The usual afternoon tea was served along with the cook's Flemish apple tart and some cookies. After waiting for the proper time, I asked to be excused so that I could play in the solarium at the rear of the house.

Walking into this room was always magic to me. Filled with light, the solarium overlooked a small, tidy garden with a birdbath in the center. Sometimes, I stood by a window and watched sparrows playfully splash and bathe. An ornate, iron plant rack was filled with pots of deep red azaleas and flowering cyclamens in beautiful shades of pink. Ruling over the solarium stood a majestic palm tree in a blue Chinese pot, with a painted, undulating dragon chasing its tail. The palm tree fascinated me. It no doubt came from a country far away. I remained as close to it as I could, sometimes lying down on the cold, black and white tile floor admiring its long, graceful fronds from beneath. I felt safe and protected.

On the table, two white cardboard boxes always awaited me. Marie-Thérèse had three grown children, and I could play with their old toys. With each visit, I seemed to discover yet another. Most were small and made of lead. There were soldiers in various uniforms, cannons, autos, and a wind-up, tin motorcycle. In addition, there were tiny celluloid dolls wearing white crocheted outfits, and a doll house with a gold Victorian miniature crib. When pushed gently, it rocked back and forth. I was *très contente*, very happy, until Mamie called from the salon, "We will be leaving shortly, *ma chérie*." With regret, I put the toys away until next time.

It was dark outside, and I was reluctant to leave the comfort and warmth of her house. In the vestibule, I felt a chill from outside. Bundled up and clutching my doll, I said, "*Merci*, Marie-Thérese. *Au revoir.*"

My grand-mère and I left, each holding a flashlight, since following German orders, most of Brussels street lights were dimmed or turned off for safety due to repeated nocturnal bombings by the British. When we turned the corner to the terminus, our tram was there waiting for us. Even with dimmed lights, it seemed so safe, reassuring, ready to take us home. And what luck! I got a window seat right away, since only a few people boarded here. Once again, feeling *très contente*, I must have dozed off, holding my doll, and feeling the packet of candy slipped in my pocket by Marie-Thérese as I kissed her, *au revoir*.

I woke-up, startled by the horrible, high-pitched sound of grinding metal, coming from beneath the tram. Forced to stop, our tram was at once boarded and taken over by six Nazi soldiers with rifles pointed at us. They were joined by three more soldiers with huge, snarling black dogs straining at their leashes.

"Oh, but look at those dogs," a woman murmured. "Even with those muzzles, they'll rip us apart."

"Ah, *oui*. Dobermans. Trained to be vicious," a man cautioned.

"Whatever happens," someone said, "try not to pass close to them."

Instinctively, I curled up my legs beneath me. It was then I caught sight of a parked truck blocking the rails. Filled with dread, I recognized it as one of those, feared green Nazi trucks. Soldiers from the truck, wearing hooded green slickers, set up barricades along the street. Other soldiers scurried back and forth trying to light red flares as a warning. I hid my face into my grandmother's side.

"Oh, Mamie, but look, look, over there. Is that truck waiting for us? Will it take us away?"

"Oh, *non, non*. It's nothing." She held me closer. I could feel her tremble. "I promise. *Non*. Nothing at all, *ma petite*."

Once we and the thirty or so passengers were searched, and all identification cards and permit papers thoroughly checked, the soldiers shouted orders for everyone to get off, their rifles pointing the way. "*Jedermann rauss. Ja. Rauss. Macht schnell.*" Get out! Hurry up!

We were lined-up against a wall in the bitter cold night. I held tight to my grand-mère's hand and we watched soldiers pace up and down, their rifles aimed at us. Suddenly, someone shouted in German. We were ordered to disperse, and walk to our separate destinations. Relieved at not being detained, but still frightened, like a flock of blackbirds, passengers scattered away in opposite directions. Instants later, all had disappeared into the darkness.

My grandmother pulled my wool hat down so far down I couldn't see. Still trembling, she wrapped her blue paisley scarf around my neck and said, as if nothing had happened, "*Et bien*, well now, let us go home, *ma chérie*."

We walked along deserted cobblestone streets, passing through dark unfamiliar neighborhoods, while I wondered whether the cost of this scary night was perhaps too high a price for an afternoon of happiness at Marie-Thérèse's. I remembered how protected I felt beneath the palm fronds just a while ago and I longed to be back in the magic of her solarium.

When my doll was placed in my grandmother's bag for another nap, I asked, "Now, please tell me. What do you think? Just how far is "our nest" now?"

"*Bientôt, ma petite. Oui bientôt.*" Soon my little one. Soon.

We walked at a brisk pace, while we sang our favorite songs to occupy our minds. By the time we sang our repertoire twice, Mamie decided to try a short cut.

"*Oui.* I think we should go this different way. It will prove very beneficial." I did not recognize this new street, but soon I heard relief in her voice. "*Et, voila! Ah, Dieu Merci!*

Thank God! Soon you will see your favorite park and our building."

There were lights ahead, and I was surprised to see the outline of the treetops in the distance. German soldiers on two motorcycles with side-cars rode by, slowed down, then parked in front of the lit building, just ahead. The four soldiers quickly marched inside the *Kommandantur*, while above the entrance a huge, red Nazi flag snapped in the bitter cold. As we approached, through the large windows I observed great activity inside. The high ceiling lights were bright, almost like daylight, so unlike our dim lights at home. Tall, grey metal cabinets lined the walls. Seated at large desks, German officers were giving orders, while handing files and documents to their staff. Two soldiers stood at attention in front of an officer speaking on a telephone. In the next room, rows of seated women dressed in the Nazi uniform, with white shirts and black neckties, were typing under the same high, clear lights. Those black neckties looked ugly, but the Nazi ladies did not seem to mind. Some were even pretty, with light blonde hair and pale skin.

The lights in the *Kommandantur* had been a welcome sight after our walk in the dark. But I was startled when, from the darkness, three men in shabby clothes, surrounded by armed soldiers, were led inside. They appeared nervous and frightened.

We passed by the steps to the wide entrance, when, just beyond the parked motorcycles, I saw the wooden cart, a *charette*, along the curb. A horse was still hitched to the cart, but he looked emaciated and ill. His front legs were giving out and the poor animal kept collapsing while trying his best to remain upright on all four legs. He was foaming at the mouth. It was a horrible sight. I slowed down wanting to pet him, to soothe him in some way, but my grand-mère held my hand tighter as two Nazi officers, speaking in German, left the building and casually strolled by. Wearing heavy military coats, their collars turned up, both men, with obvious pleasure, were smoking. While the stocky, older officer puffed on a distinctive, fine German pipe, the other, slowly exhaled smoke from a cigarette. The unexpected, pleasant smell of rich tobacco soon drifted into the crisp night air.

For an instant, I caught a glimpse of something dark and shiny in the younger officer's coarse leather-gloved hand. My grandmother whispered, "Don't turn around, *ma chérie*, look ahead." Moments later, still pursued by the now faint aroma of tobacco, we reached the end of the street. "Look! *Voila*, your park!" We turned the corner, and there it was. Now I knew we would be home soon, for I could see the outline of our building in the distance beyond the tree tops.

"But, Mamie, tell me. What happened to that horse? Why is he so *fatigué?*"

She paused for a moment. "He probably has traveled a long distance."

"Will he soon be getting his hay and perhaps a carrot, since he has been so brave?"

She did not reply. Instead, suddenly humming *La Marseillaise*, she accelerated our steps. Now almost running along Quai à la Houille, I saw tears on her flushed cheeks. "I think they will take care of him very soon, *ma petite.*"

But I did not believe her. An instant later, I heard the single, sharp crack of a gunshot behind us.

"There, *ma chérie*," she whispered. "There. Now the poor horse will never have to suffer again."

Later that evening, when my doll Suzette and I were warm and safe in my bed, I heard the gun shot sound again and again, and I cried. I yearned to go back and pet him, to tell him he was a good and faithful horse. I vowed I would never again walk on Rue du Canal and I never did. It took me a long time to fall asleep that night, and I woke up late the next morning.

My grandmother and I never spoke of that day again. Not even with my grandfather.

Descent into Darkness
February 1944

It always began at night, with the wailing of sirens warning us of impending bombings. The mad scrambling before the black-out for our robes, coats, mufflers, and warm socks, all slipped on as our multiple fears escalated. Together, we rushed from our tenth-floor nest to begin the long descent to safety in the cold, foreboding basement. The elevator was already busy on lower floors, so holding flashlights, our journey began on foot down the dark stairwell. But, we were not alone. Our tall, persistent, shadows accompanied us along the cold, stone walls of the stairwells. Floor after floor, they followed us with silent determination. They scared me. Each time, as we reached the next landing, I glanced back, hoping they would give up and disappear. But they did not. At some point, arriving on a lower level, as we joined and waited with the anxious tenants who lived on that floor for a ride to the basement, only then did they give up and vanish.

In the elevator, I avoided looking at anything

by huddling into the sides of my grandmother's robe, pretending this was not really happening. More people waited as we passed lower floors, but the elevator was full. Heavily loaded with passengers, it continued its downward journey, passing by landings where frowning, impatient people stood waiting. Their murmured hostilities, sometimes a shouted, angry comment, could be heard as the sluggish, burdened, elevator headed toward its basement destination, oblivious to the unhappiness it was causing.

Once we reached the dark, musty cellar, we filed out and headed to our cubicle. These small storage rooms, doors padlocked by owners, were assigned individually to each apartment. Ours was the last at the end of a long row, closest to the main street entrance directly above. We walked in single file along the narrow maze of aisles. Tenants who arrived earlier had already set up low-wooden benches, or sometimes, bright-striped, canvas beach stools and, as we walked by, they sat in front of their cubicles, chatting in low voices: the women in long robes, their hair in curlers and wrapped in scarves, the men, usually smoking, often wore coats instead of robes over their pajamas. Their prying eyes watched our arrival. I sensed tension among neighbors. No one trusted anyone. The colorful beach stools seemed so out of place in this sad, dank basement, far away from their original intended purpose on sunny, distant beaches.

My grandfather unlocked the door to our room, filled with suitcases, a trunk, a narrow bench and a coal bin, that took up a quarter of the floor space. As soon as he shuffled the suitcases and opened the folding chairs, we tried to settle in with blankets and pillows we had brought down with us. While my grandparents and Juliette were busy preparing for the long night ahead, I would peek from behind the open door, sometimes even stand outside and watch the curious activity taking place in the cubicle across from ours.

It belonged to a couple who had recently moved into the building. They lived on the third floor. She always wore a red-fox fur coat over her long, royal blue velvet robe, and blue, high-heeled slippers on her dainty, pedicured feet. Sometimes a matching red-fox hat was perched on top of her bouncy red curls. This unusual combination seemed odd, but nothing on these fragmented, scary, nights made sense to me. I was fascinated by their attempt to create some pleasure and comfort in their private space. They both sat on high-backed, wooden chairs facing each other, with a small crate set between them. Before sitting, the woman produced several items from her large, brown leather bag, placed them on a wide shelf on the back wall. She then lit a single candle in a blue, enameled holder. Instantly, the musty cubicle took on a softer glow. She would unfold an immaculate, white embroidered, linen napkin, and place it on top of the low crate. Two champagne glasses would appear, followed by small, delicate sandwiches, which, once unwrapped, she placed on a round tray. While he, standing in the far corner of the room, opened a bottle of cold champagne, which he cautiously held underneath a folded blanket to help muffle the unmistakable popping sound of the cork. I was spellbound, yet also reassured by this unusual routine during these dark, frightening nights.

Too soon my grand-mère warned me, "Françoise! Ah, la, la, stop. Stop staring, *ma petite*, and come inside. *Immédiatement.*"

By then they were sitting down, having their first sip of cold champagne, facing each other, pretending they were elsewhere. I admired them, but other neighbors looked at them with suspicion and envy, as they only brought thermoses of coffee and chunks of coarse bread and cheese. Sometimes a few came with just sandwiches and bottles of Belgian beer.

Back inside our space, I tried sleeping on the bench with my head resting on Mamie's lap as she sang my favorite songs. Other times I would climb on top of the suitcases and fall asleep with my pillow and a blanket over me. This could last for a couple of hours or more, but sometimes it would be daylight before the sirens would sound again, this time announcing the end of the air raid. But during the nights when bombs fell nearby, the thunderous sound of the first explosion woke me with a frightening start. Soon another explosion would follow. Then another, and another, each blast sounding farther away. And so these too, these heavy, relentless, bombardments, always the same, became a routine part of the nocturnal chaos.

"It is nothing, *ma petite chérie*," my grandmother calmly whispered, "just close your eyes now and go back to sleep.

Soon, *oui, oui,* very soon it will all be over."

I tried. I wanted to, but I did not believe her. The constant, repetitive sound of bombings instilled my fear and conviction of more yet to come. Trying to fall back asleep, my head under the blue, scratchy wool blanket, I wondered what giant force was outside punishing us in the darkness of night? What had we done to cause such powerful anger?

One night, as the familiar sirens began their shrill warning, things changed dramatically. My grandmother announced she would no longer go to the basement, but remain instead in our apartment, surrounded by her books and the paintings she loved.

"If a bomb should hit our complex," she explained, "we will be trapped under the rubble of a ten-story apartment building and perish slowly without any air, food, or water. You see, Alex, *mon cher,* this exact tragedy has taken place recently in London just a few days ago and was reported in yesterday's newspaper."

"*Ah, Mon Dieu!* Please be reasonable, Alice," Papy begged, horrified.

"*Non, non, non.* It's over, Alex. I just can't anymore. That's enough. Please forgive me." And as the relentless, alarming sounds of sirens tore into the night, she turned and walked away to their bedroom.

Shaken, he reluctantly led Juliette and me for our descent into darkness.

"Mamie, come with us! Mamie!"

But Juliette held my hand. "Oh, please! Stop crying and just think about the steps. Be careful. Don't fall down."

Ahead of us, in the black stairwell, my grandfather, flashlight in hand, sounded bewildered, as with every other step he repeated her name.

"Alice, Alice, *ah, la, la, Mon Dieu*. Oh, Alice. Ah, what a disaster." When at last we caught up with the elevator for our journey down below, I saw a tear roll down his unshaven face.

It was on that cold night, huddled against Juliette in the dark, that, for the first time, reality appeared before me. Cloaked in horror, it whispered its simple revelation. I listened, and I finally understood.

Death. It was death. We were hoping to escape death by hiding in the basement. Quite simply, we could all be dead within an instant. Poof. Dead. *La fin*. The end. Then what? Would it hurt? Would our own angels lift us out of the scary basement to arrive up in heaven moments later? Would Little Jesus greet each of us, give us our own cloud to sit on? Would we then be safe amidst floating angels playing music, like the paintings in church and at the museums? Troubled, I thought about all this most of the night, but I had just one more question. I tried waking up Juliette for an answer.

"*Ah, non*," she mumbled. "Just go back to sleep."

I wanted to ask Papy, but he was snoring in the far corner of our cubicle. So, I drifted off to sleep pondering the same things over and over. If the bomb fell and we died, would we arrive in heaven still dressed in our pajamas? Would the ladies still have their hair in curlers? Or would we be wearing beautiful white robes? In the morning, if I could remember it all, I would get my answers.

Daylight was breaking as we returned to our tenth-floor nest. Mamie was reading in bed. She seemed calm. We ran and kissed her. Papy held her for a few moments in his arms whispering, "Alice, *ma chère*, Alice. Ah, thank God!"

As Juliette headed to the kitchen to make coffee and toast for everyone, she repeated while crossing herself, "Ah, Madame, Madame. *Ah, oui*, thank God!"

I knew right there and then that my grand-mère was right. The descent into darkness was not our salvation. It was the last time we went to the sinister basement. My grand-père refused to go without her at his side. I, too, refused to go without her, and having thought it over, felt if we were to die suddenly, it made perfect sense to have it happen in "our nest", surrounded by the things we loved rather than in the foreboding, cold basement with strangers. Juliette still went down, however, as she felt it her civic duty to do what had officially been asked of all citizens by the authorities. Besides, she believed the basement was still a safer place to be during the bombardments. From then on, during nocturnal air raids, I spent the nights in Mamie's warm bed, right next to her.

But, before the blackout, I created a ritual for myself. Once safe under her yellow, quilted, satin comforter, holding both my doll and my teddy bear just in case we all went to heaven that night, before I closed my eyes, I looked first at my favorite painting of a beach scene hanging above Mamie's desk. Then, I gazed at her porcelain lamp, the one with the painted bird and flower, its tiny bulb, and the pink, silk shade which, for the next moments, still bathed the room in a soft, reassuring, glow. I took in all this visual beauty, realizing it truly was the best way to leave this world, knowing that the last things I had enjoyed looking at were beautiful. And should a bomb hit us, the next thing my eyes would see would be serene heaven, angels and Little Jesus. Having perfected this ritual, over a period of time, I managed to fall asleep almost immediately, feeling safer here now than anywhere else on earth. My previous fears had disappeared, though at times during the night, I heard my grandfather praying in his bed next to us.

The Little Dog
April 12, 1944

Earlier than usual, I left my doll and the warmth of my bed, and tip-toed past Juliette, still sleeping and slightly snoring with that soft, purring sound of hers. Gripping the flashlight always kept by my bedside, I entered the cold, dark kitchen and quietly moved the yellow stool to beneath the calendar. I needed confirmatiêon that today was the special, long awaited Wednesday.

Using the stove for support, I climbed up and looked again at the red circle drawn by my grandfather around Wednesday, April 12, and below his neat handwriting, in blue ink: Le Pérruchêt Children's Theater 2 p.m. Reassured, I moved the stool back too quickly. It made a scraping sound on the kitchen tiles. Afraid of waking Juliette, I ran back to my bed. Snuggled under the covers with my doll I whispered, "Today is going to be spectacular!"

Juliette stirred and mumbled. "Another ten minutes would be nice."

I agreed.

At twelve-forty-five, my punctual grand-père and I left for our monthly Wednesday matinee in Schaerbeek. This was our special time together. I felt quite grown up, and with my grandfather holding my hand, our tram ride was always a safe, pleasant routine. We had a fifteen-minute walk, during which he often spoke of his childhood, his schooling with the Jesuit priests, his early love of drawing, and getting in trouble for drawing caricatures during algebra lessons. Sometimes my grand-père mentioned his life in Paris at the turn of the century. While a student, he worked as one of the many extras at the Paris Opéra, thereby enjoying performances from behind the scenes. He spoke of the many artists, the elegant women, the crowded boulevards.

My excitement grew as we reached Boulevard Lambermont, lined with older, stately homes. Two blocks away on a side street, was our destination: Le Pérruchêt Children's Theater. But today, as we neared the corner, everything was different. People gathered in front of what had been three large houses where, we were told, two days ago a bomb fell during a night raid by the British. Their mission was to damage the nearby railway line, vital to the Germans' ability to deliver and control supplies to their troops. This type of bombing was done at night on a regular basis. Often from our tenth-floor balcony, miles away across Brussels, we saw the glare of bombs hitting their selected targets in Schaerbeek. But, two nights ago they missed and instead demolished these older, stone residences.

Today nothing remained standing except a large portion of an ornate, black grilled gate, its base hidden in a pile of smoldering debris. Defiantly still standing, the gate, a tall, black silhouette, sharply set against mounds of limestone chunks, appeared to be vainly trying to still protect the entrance to its former, elegant home, as it had for the last sixty years, or more. I noticed, with apprehension, a man foraging through the dangerous glass shards and chunks of broken stone. What could he be searching for? Everything was gone. Pulverized.

What happened to the occupants? Had they fled in time? I looked in vain for remaining traces of the bow window where a small grey and white dog would sit watching the passersby. We had a regular routine as he recognized me and enjoyed watching me walk by. Wagging his tail, he jumped up and down barking. I imitated him, jumping up and down waving my arms until his owner, a tall, grey-haired lady with jeweled bracelets on her thin wrists, wearing grey or mauve silky sweaters, picked him up and carried him away from the window, kissing and admonishing him. Led away by Papy, I was scolded as well.

This afternoon, all that remained was indescribable stone and twisted rubble. In silence, holding hands, we turned the corner and headed toward the theater.

Near the entrance I asked, "Tell me, Papy. What do you think happened to the people and to my friend, the little dog?"

He did not answer right away, but as we walked, still hand-in-hand into Le Pérruchêt's dark, red-striped lobby, he tried to explain. "Ah, well, there you see, *ma petite*, what luck! They are away on vacation."

"Where?"

"Ah, *ma chérie*, but the Riviera, of course," he said with a sad smile. He paused, then whispered. "Ah, *oui*, the Riviera."

I was relieved, but felt sorry for what awaited them upon their return.

Magical Woods
1942-1944

A magical place, only an hour away from where we lived, Le Bois de la Cambre was easily reached by tram. This world of nature was so different, that the time we spent there filled me with wonder. Our planned destination set, my grandmother and I, sometimes with my grandfather, would enter, with awe, this cool, enchanted world of ancient oak trees, some more than a hundred years old. As we followed the walking paths lining curved, paved roads, we enjoyed the earthy wood essences while guessing what species of birds we heard in the trees, amused by and sometimes startled by squirrels jumping from branch to branch above our heads. We spotted rabbits and, at times, several graceful, fleeing deer in the distance. A twenty-minute walk led us to a calm lake, with a small island in the center. Because it was accessed only by boat, it seemed remote and mysterious to me. The silence and stillness of the lake was disturbed only by the monotonous croaking sounds of frogs, and ducks gracefully swooping into the dark water.

Bois de la Cambre, the magical woods, after the war.

At the edge of the lake, brightly painted rowboats bobbed alongside narrow wooden docks. The smell of fresh varnish escaped from their sunbaked, glossy wood interiors. With large, individual, black numbers painted on their side, they waited to be rented. The man in charge sat inside a colorful, striped, wood kiosk painted with the same colors as the boats. Seated before an open window, he enjoyed a panoramic view of the lake, greeted people, then led them to their chosen boat. He wore a flat-top straw hat and carried a brown leather bag strapped around his middle in which he placed francs collected for the rentals. When idle, he sat inside reading his newspaper, sometimes eating a sandwich. He seemed to have a pleasant life, living in his small, striped kiosk by the peaceful lake. I envied him and thought, perhaps one day, I might do the same.

Beyond the boating area was an outdoor café. As we approached the tables, set beneath green umbrellas, we encountered a familiar aroma, the strong, chicory-blended coffee, being served to a few relaxed patrons. Sandwiches were available along with the café's cherry tart, their aptly named specialty. Due to the shortage of sugar needed in its preparation, it tasted sour. After a few minutes, once excused, I would run to the swings. It was then the best part of the day began.

During the war, people with children were fearful. They preferred staying close to home and the four swings were always empty. I chose my favorite, the second one from the right. There was no thrill like flying up high, that soaring feeling of freedom. While up in the air, I spotted ducks and swans taking their naps nestled among reeds bordering the lake. Further away, a few scattered, lazy rowboats drifted on the still water. When I swung even higher, I got a better view of the small, wooded, island across the lake, hoping perhaps to get a glimpse of the white unicorn that, I was told, lived there.

Late in the afternoon, the dark, glossy, green-headed ducks and elegant white swans gathered along the narrow shores of the lake. We always brought our left-over bread and fed them, but the swans were aggressive and scared me. They ruled the lake and, once fed, would silently glide away in pairs, their piercing, sharp, black eyes accentuated by the yellow orange of their beaks. When my grandfather came, he rented a boat, and together we explored the lake and edges of the island. Trailing my hand in the water, I was intrigued by the strange pungent smell of decaying vegetation along these low wooded areas. I felt certain that, beside the visible fish, frogs, birds, rabbits and squirrels, my invisible friends, the fairies and mystical creatures were, in turn, curiously watching us drift by their magical woods.

Away from the city surrounded by the silent, healing power of the majestic woods, these few hours' promenades always nurtured us. Riding home on the tram, still embraced by this magic solace, its healing remained with us for the next few days.

Promenade Interrompue
May 1944

Aware of my excitement and impatience, my grandparents waited until supper to tell me of a planned excursion to visit the magical woods set for tomorrow afternoon. Later, as we kissed good-night, I reminded my grandmother, "Oh, please don't forget the stale, left-over bread for the swans and ducks. Perhaps you could put it in your purse now, just in case? Oh, but I am so happy, I can't wait until tomorrow!"

As I fell asleep, I was *très contente* and thought of all the wonders this ancient forest held for me. This enormous, green cathedral, a world of nature so different from the city, filled me with awe. Would we be lucky tomorrow and see the fleeing deer again? I thought of the hungry swans and ducks waiting for us at the edge of the dark, silent lake. I also knew my invisible friends, the fairies and mystical creatures, would be there in the woods, looking for me.

The following afternoon, a spring day in May, as my grand-mere and I walked toward the lake, a black car flying the red Nazi flags zoomed passed us. Someone on the foot path was walking in our direction, a German soldier, with a rifle strapped on his shoulder. His jacket was ill-fitting, too large for his body. I stopped, afraid, but *grand-mère* took my hand. "Ah, *ma chérie,* he will not hurt us. Why, he's only a lad. *Ah, oui,* look. He's just a youth."

"*Guten tag,*" she said as we passed each other. He barely nodded, looked straight ahead and with a determined military step, continued to strut away. I turned around just as he adjusted the rifle strap over his narrow shoulder.

"Oh, Mamie, but you said good day to the enemy. Why?"

"Oh, well, why not, *ma chérie?* It is such a beautiful afternoon, and it seems the right thing to do."

But I remained apprehensive.

When we came upon a barricade blocking cars from continuing further into the park, I realized today things were not the same. Since the footpath was not blocked, we continued our promenade, teased by gentle spring breezes. Above us, trees showed off their new, delicate, leaves. A rabbit hopped away among young uncurling ferns.

We approached the familiar steep ravine in the clearing across the road, but today Nazi military trucks, those familiar, scary green trucks, were parked on the side by the scrubby shrubs. Hundreds of bareheaded German soldiers, some in white undershirts, but most bare-chested, swarmed over the usually empty, grass-covered clearing. They were everywhere. Volley ball nets were set up and soldiers played with enthusiasm. Others sat on blankets, picnicking and relaxing. Many sang along while standing soldiers played their accordions. Just as sounds of their unfamiliar German songs reached our ears, I stopped to stare at an incredible sight.

Motorcycles started racing in the ravine. Amazed by the maneuvering skills and daredevil stunts, we stared in disbelief. Three motorcyclists, starting at the top of the ravine, raced to the bottom as the crowd cheered. Once they reached the bottom, three more would repeat this feat, while on the far side of the hill the ones who had finished, maneuvered their heavy motorcycles, a few even with sidecars, back up the steep hill before they once again raced down the treacherous ravine. The incessant roar of thirty or more motorcycles was deafening.

I was stunned, overwhelmed, not only by this extraordinary spectacle, but by the wholesome appearance of these German soldiers. Without their military jackets, caps, or menacing guns, hundreds of these feared Nazis were playing games and enjoying themselves. Since most were blond and fair skinned, many were already sunburned by the May sun. The contrast between these vibrant Germans, full of life, and the pale, fearful Belgian people I saw every day, was shocking.

I sensed danger, and the heavy, odd thumping sound of their music added to my fear. "I'm so scared! Oh, please, please, I really am. I hope they're so busy playing, they won't notice us walking by."

"But it's perfectly all right, *ma petite*. Besides, don't forget your friends, the ducks and swans, are waiting for us." We continued until we rounded a bend and then we saw it. A red metal sign hung from a barrier across the road. Its bold black letters read: **Verboten!**

Darting from the underbrush, twenty yards away, a German soldier on patrol took the rifle off his shoulder, pointed it toward us and shouted in anger.

"*Rauss! Schnell, schnell!*" And he chased us.

We ran holding hands. Out of breath, and filled with fear I looked over my shoulder several times to make sure he was no longer behind us. When my grand-mère's tortoise-shell hairpin fell out, it was the first time I saw her chignon come undone. Her face was flushed, and she appeared shaken. Her mauve scarf had slipped away. It lay behind us, on the ground.

"*Oh, non, ma petite!* Leave it. Please *non!* Oh, don't go back!" But I ran and retrieved it for her. I had to. It was her favorite.

Hearts pounding, we reached the exit gate. She borrowed one of my barrettes for her chignon, then retied the ribbons on my braids. Our *promenade interrompue*, before we left the park, I chose the most venerable, ancient oak tree, the one with a bronze plaque, closest to the gate, and emptied the bag of bread crumbs around its base, knowing the birds and squirrels would find them. Through branches above a slight breeze whispered, "Stay. Don't leave. Please come back and play."

Seated beside Mamie on the moving tram, it took several minutes before, still clinging to her, I dared to look back, petrified that one of those green Nazi trucks might be following us with orders to take us away, as they had Marcel.

During the remainder of our ride home, my head resting on my grand-mère's arm, I stared at the flowers on her mauve scarf and I understood. Today, the Nazis had invaded my magical woods. Its once healing solace and tranquility was now trampled. It would never again be the same. For, as of today, fear ruled there, too.

The rhythmic refrain of metal wheels repeating, "Never the same, never the same, never the same."

Safe from The Madness
September 2, 1944

The familiar yellow trams of Brussels were scarce that Saturday. After waiting more than twenty minutes at Place de la Bourse, determined to maintain our ritual of required presence for the one o'clock Saturday dinner at his parents, my father decided we would walk there.

At once my mother smiled and agreed. "Oh, *oui!* Why not? It's such a beautiful, late summer day!"

Only a few people were out walking, unlike other Saturdays when streets and boulevards were crowded with people leisurely strolling along. I found this unsettling. We trudged our way up the steep, narrow Rue de la Madeleine, lined with ancient, two or three storied buildings, old bookstores, and former antique shops, once filled with desirable, prized merchandise. Today, their facades were closed, hidden behind heavy metal shutters, or thick, padlocked, grilled gates, giving the sunless street a feeling of desolation. I was told their owners, mostly Jewish, had "moved away."

We passed the Chapelle de la Madeleine where a life-sized statue of Jesus as a blond young child wearing a long pink dress had always fascinated me. At last, the dreary street ended at a wide roundabout. Within moments the sun warmed our bodies. Uphill, I could see Montagne de la Caudenberg's terraced gardens and its bordering cobblestone street where we were headed. Then I noticed a thin, black plume of smoke, high on the right of the horizon.

"Maman, Papa. Look! There's something in the sky! *Mais regardez*. But look. Oh, please, look up. Over there!" But, my parents walked on. Engrossed in conversation they ignored me. I ran up and tugged at my mother's arm. Surprised, they stopped, listened, then looked up. Speechless, we just stared. The plume grew a bit wider. Encouraged by the wind, it soon became thicker. Small red flames began to dance in and out of the black smoke.

My father exploded in anger. "Ah, *Nom de Dieu*. In God's name, it's our Palais de Justice! Ah, *Sacrebleu*! How can it be on fire?"

Brussels' magnificent Palais de Justice stood on a hill overlooking the older part of the city. World famous, built in the late nineteenth century, it was one of the world's largest buildings – larger than St. Peter's Basilica in Rome.

We stood, hypnotized on the sidewalk, when the unexpected, thunderous sound of motorcycles startled us. Across from us, just twenty feet away, from a major

The Palace of Justice as I first saw it.

Later that day.

underground bunker beneath the roundabout, German troops emerged on their motorcycles into the sunlight and rode up the steep hill toward the Palais de Justice and the fire. In silence I stood between my mother and father. Why? Why of all the streets in Brussels had we taken this one? The roar of motorcycles became deafening, as now they came out three abreast, each side-car filled with a soldier, piled with luggage and cartons.

His fist clenched, my father shouted, "*Sacrebleu!* But they're all leaving! *Ah, Nom de Dieu, ils foutrent le camp,* they're fleeing! *Ah, quels salauds,* they're running away — back to their godforsaken *Deutschland uber alles!!*"

Long black cars emerged, flying the red Nazi flag on both sides of their windshields. Crowded together, sitting rigid, Nazi officers filled the cars, drivers taking orders from the officers inside. When traffic congestion stopped the flow of emerging cars, one of the more luxurious automobiles came to a stop close to where we stood. Inside, three Nazi officers sat together in the plush back seat. One became agitated. Gesturing, he leaned forward and shouted to his sergeant and driver. Both men nodded and looked straight ahead. From a briefcase on his lap, the second officer, who sat in the middle and appeared calm, produced a map, which all three, using hand-held magnifying glasses, studied with great care. They discussed their decision before marking the map using their fountain pens. The first portly one leaned forward again and through the open, glass partition pointed to the map, yelling instructions to the driver. The third officer, the one sitting closest to where I stood, was thin, and wore round-rimmed glasses. Exasperated, he removed his military hat and wiped his brow. Nearly bald, his remaining few strands of hair were neatly parted. When he caught me staring, his sharp beady eyes narrowed. I feared he was going to give the order and have me killed right there. Instead, he glared down with contempt. Then, with great military precision he replaced his hat, stiffened his back, raised his head higher and stared straight ahead. The car drove on, just as a glimmer of sunlight passed through the rear windows down to where I stood.

Smaller black cars followed carrying lower ranking officers and staff. Soldiers on foot, carrying bags and bundles, came running out. The last ones to leave, they were agitated, flagging down cars for a ride, shouting amongst themselves, "*Ach, schnell. Rauss, sogleich! Ach, machen schnell.*" Ah, fast. Out, immediately. Ah, make it fast! Chasing behind, they climbed on running-boards, and clung to the sides of fleeing cars. After a few moments, only four or five more motorcycles trickled out, picked up the last two men running and rode away, up the steep, cobblestone hill, past the terraced gardens. The three of us remained, frozen in disbelief, watching our powerful conquerors suddenly fleeing our city in panic.

Then, it became eerily quiet. Motorcycle and automobile fumes lingered in the air. Abandoned, half-open cartons of documents and files, tossed at the last moments from sidecars, littered the sidewalk. A single, grey military cap, with the red Nazi emblem on the peak, lay in the gutter. My parents hesitated. They both seemed lost until my mother ventured, "Should we perhaps turn back and go home?"

In a daze my father, replied in a low voice, "Ah, *oui*, certainly. Why not?"

Paralyzed with fear, I was angry with my father. Why had we waited so long? We were not invisible, the three of us standing on that sidewalk. The Germans could have shot us as revenge for their having to flee! It was my father's earlier decision to have us walk across Brussels for a dinner at his parents' home. He had placed us in harm's way.

During our fast walk home along the now deserted streets, the magnitude of this destructive act became clear. My parents discussed that Hitler was so fond of our Palais that he ordered his architect, Albert Speer, to design several monumental buildings in Nazi Germany based on the Belgian design.

"The Nazis probably set the fire on the Fuhrer's orders," my father said. "Their last, vengeful deed of hatred, before retreating to Germany."

We returned to the tenth-floor nest, and were greeted with relief by my maternal grandparents and Juliette. An earlier newscast had been sketchy, but rumors indicated that the Allies were, at this very moment, heading toward Brussels.

With a smile, Mamie announced, "An impromptu *déjeuner*, will be served shortly," as she and my mother selected a few canned goods from the meager provisions in the bottom of our dining room buffet. Apparently successful, they disappeared in the kitchen and joined Juliette, improvising a larger meal. I was told, "Be ready to help set the table."

My father telephoned his parents to explain the events of the fire and the Nazi's frantic, disorganized retreat, while my grandfather stood on our terrace with his binoculars, calling for us to join him and see the Palais de Justice now completely enveloped in angry, black, billowing smoke.

Moments later, his voice breaking with emotion, he announced "Ah, *mes enfants, quel désastre!* What a disaster! Ah, *non!* Come and look! Ah, *mon Dieu!* A portion of the copper dome has just collapsed!" This confirmed my father's earlier fear and suspicion.

I stood next to my grandfather on our balcony, and took one last look at the dark, smoke-filled sky above Brussels. Stunned by the enormous destructive force of the fire I had first noticed only two hours ago, when it first began, I turned away.

Slowly I walked to the opposite side of the apartment. I thought about the events of this morning. Still in awe, I recalled how thin and almost pretty the black smoke ribbon was when it first appeared. Then, how rapidly it unfurled its dark, ominous power in the blue September sky. I entered my room, closed the door behind me and climbed up on my bed. I picked up my doll and I whispered, "Oh, how lucky you are to have stayed home today."

I lay on the bed, and holding her close, at last felt safe

from the madness. As the afternoon sunlight filled my room, it slowly enveloped me with its reassuring warmth.

Les Beaux Drapeaux
September 3, 1944

I woke up the day after seeing the fire set by the fleeing Germans, to the sharp sound of gunshots coming from the streets below. Thinking that, perhaps, I was dreaming, I held my doll and sank deeper under the down comforter where the faint, familiar, lingering scent of starch on the fresh sheets, made everything feel safe and normal. Outside, the shots continued, but not as frequently.

I smelled coffee and toast and heard my grandparents in the kitchen, but it seemed earlier than usual. In the dim light, I noticed Juliette standing on a stool in the corner of my room, taking something from the top of the *armoire*. I wasn't ready to get up, and from the warmth of my bed, I watched her unfold then inspect a bed sheet. It seemed odd.

"*Bonjour* Juliette, what are you doing?"

"*Ah, bonjour ma petite. Ah, oui*, today is a great day! We're going to make *des beaux drapeaux*, beautiful flags. The Allies are coming and *les sales Boches* are fleeing! *Vive la*

Belgique!"

Her happiness was contagious. I followed her into our brightly lit, yellow kitchen. "*Oh*, Madame, look, I found this one," she said. "It is perfect." My grandmother agreed that it could indeed be cut and made into flags. "*Des beaux drapeaux!*" Juliette continued. "Strung across our balcony. *Oh, oui,* Madame, you'll see it will be *magnifique!*"

Ten stories below, shots were still being fired. I sensed Mamie's distress. Her hands shook. She dropped the sugar bowl, but it didn't break. My grandfather walked to the other end of the apartment and turned on the radio.

"But, why are we all up?" I asked. "Why so early this morning? And why are there gunshots in the street?"

In a halting voice my grandmother replied, "Ah, *ma petite,* the Allies have liberated Antwerp and they're apparently heading toward Brussels right now, but not all German troops have left. The Gestapo is still patrolling. Even streets downstairs. So far nothing is definite yet." She hugged me and sighed. "Ah, *Mon Dieu, non. Non, ma pauvre chérie, non,* not just yet."

Juliette, oblivious to my grand-mère's precautionary outlook, was looking for the scissors in the kitchen drawer, humming, *La Brabançonne,* the regal, Belgian national anthem.

From the salon, my grand-père called my grandmother, who spoke English. The BBC began broadcasting news. But the quality of the broadcast was not very clear, interspersed at times with erratic crackling, shrill, whistling sounds.

I finished my breakfast in the kitchen as Juliette cut the white sheet into perfect rectangles. She counted them before placing them in four piles on the kitchen table, then announced: "This morning, at eight o'clock, we'll run downstairs to Monsieur Vande Putte's Hardware Store, buy little boxes of dye, come right back upstairs and make our *beaux drapeaux. Vive la Libération!* You'll see, *ma petite, ah, oui,* we'll soon be free again!"

In the salon, the dark, velvet plum drapes were still drawn, the pale, celadon-green lamp, next to the radio offered the only light, giving the room a cloistered atmosphere. "It's for the best, *ma chérie.* Much safer I think," Papy confided.

Feeling uneasy, as I realized today things were changing around us, I walked back to the kitchen and watched Juliette rummage in the bottom of the kitchen cabinets to successfully produce three old cooking pots. But she needed a fourth. Kneeling and searching a bit more, she found another and was now looking for worn wooden spoons. She placed the worst looking ones in the water-filled pots then exclaimed, "*Voila,* it's all ready!" It was only six-thirty. We had an hour and a half before Monsieur Vande Putte opened his door. We got dressed and I helped Juliette put the breakfast dishes away. The gunshots had stopped. Where had they gone?

At twenty minutes to eight, Juliette asked for a few francs to buy the boxes of dye. My grandmother refused. "Ah, *non.* Absolutely not. It is much too dangerous still to venture outside."

Juliette insisted. She had a plan. Now, of course, she would go alone, use the back entrance to the walled-in court yard below, re-enter the other section of our apartment complex, walk out using that front door, step outside, turn left and *voila*, she would be at the entrance of the hardware store where, "I will *vite, vite,* buy the essential boxes of dye then in just a few minutes. I'll return here the same way."

She was relentless, until my grandfather shouted, "*Ah, Mon Dieu,* that's enough. *Sapristi!* Go ahead then, if you please!" Holding the few francs in her hand, humming *La Brabançonne* under her breath, Juliette rushed out on her mission. In less than twenty minutes she returned, proud of her successful purchase.

"*Oh, la, la,* Madame, so many people will be making flags today! The shop is jammed with customers and the boxes of dye are disappearing from the wooden shelves. Why, there were only three boxes of red dye by the time I left. *Oh, oui,* truly Madame, we're lucky to now have these to create our *beaux drapeaux.*"

My grandmother suggested, "The soup should be prepared now, so that the dyeing process not interfere with *le déjeuner* being served exactly at noon, as usual."

"*Oui,* Madame, absolutely. *Oui, une très bonne idée!*"

I sat in the kitchen and kept her company as she peeled vegetables. She placed them in a large, yellow, cast-iron pot and started their slow simmering. We each ate a carrot and together sang *La Brabançonne.* My favorite and most inspiring part was the finale with its three successive repeats of "*Le Roi, La Loi, La Liberté,*" The King, The Law, and Liberty. Later that morning, I went back to the salon and asked Papy to teach me the French national anthem, *La Marseillaise*. He did, and I found it more stirring than *La Brabançonne*, since he added his own interesting drum-roll sounds between each verse.

From their nearby apartment, my parents called and thought it best, as things were changing fast, to come over and all be together. My father was certain they could make it by following along the narrow back streets behind our neighboring apartment buildings. We waited, anxious with fear, but with their safe arrival half an hour later, our tenth-floor nest was full. The gunshots had stopped, and the plum drapes were drawn open by my grandfather.

It was a sunny Sunday morning, although a large portion of the September sky above Brussels held lingering powerful traces of yesterday's dark clouds of smoke. Today, huge monotonous grey clouds remained in the distance, floating with persistence above the Palais de Justice, a sad reminder of yesterday's vengeful deed by the fleeing Nazis. These lingering, motionless clouds seemed to yet emphasize the magnitude of their parting, destructive act. Still standing today, the smoldering Palais was missing its familiar, magnificent copper dome, now vanished, and reduced to ashes. In the distance the once imposing Palais appeared wounded, reminding me of a large, soft-boiled egg, with its top neatly sheared off.

In the kitchen the soup was simmering, waiting for noon to strike on the living room mantle-clock. Juliette was busy stirring the pots of dye, making certain the white rectangles were turning black, yellow, and red. In the back row there was a fourth, the blue pot, for the creation of the French flags.

I disliked the steamy odor of boiling dyes, and went to my room from where I heard Juliette, satisfied with her creations, calling for my grandmother, who replied, "*Très bien*, I will begin to make *les drapeaux*."

The colored pieces were rolled in old towels, placed in front of the portable electric heater, then ironed by my mother. Mamie set up her sewing machine and began the task of turning the colored rectangles into flags, each with a narrow sleeve at the top. My grandfather produced a long, sturdy rope, and soon, we all stood, admiring a long string of small, alternating, blue, white and red French flags, and the black, yellow and red Belgian flags. It was quite festive, but my grandfather cautioned, "Ah, *non*, we best wait. It is much too soon to risk hanging them from the balcony. The last German troops may be still patrolling and if the Gestapo sees our flags, we'll all be arrested." My father thought the same. So, for now, we hung them across the dining room. It was like a party!

At precisely noon, as our clock on the mantelpiece chimed its familiar, light, twelve crystalline notes, my grandfather stood at the head of our dining table and offered a solemn toast.

"To the spirit of the Belgian and French people, who will soon be free and greet the Allies, who have come so valiantly from far away, across the vast ocean, leaving their loved ones behind to save us from the dark, oppressive years of Nazi occupation."

Upon hearing these moving words, my mother, grandmother and Juliette burst into uncontrollable sobs. Within moments, Juliette, embarrassed, ran back to the kitchen.

My father then stood up. Holding up his glass he said, "Hail to our Nation. Long live *la Belgique!*" Then, added, "The soup should be served while hot, not lukewarm. Let us proceed with *le déjeuner.*"

Looking up above our table with admiration, I exclaimed, "Ah, *les beaux drapeaux!*"

Liberation Day
September 3, 1944

After lunch, as coffee was being served, gunshots rang out. The same sounds that woke me this morning were heard once again. But this time, standing together on our balcony as my grandfather adjusted his binoculars, we stared captivated by the events unfolding ten stories below.

From the low corner building across the street, white puffs of gun smoke were visible coming from a second-floor window. To our left, running out of the park, was a group of seven civilians armed with pistols and rifles pointed toward the building.

My father exclaimed, "Ah, *Nom de Dieu!* See their armbands? It's *la Résistance! Ah, Sacrebleu!* Look! One is a woman!"

Two of the men knelt down and began shooting toward the window. Hearing that a woman was fighting alongside these daring men, I asked for a turn to look through the binoculars. My grand-père agreed, and adjusted them for

Grand-père on our terrace a few years before the
war. Look at the building on the right side of the
photo, and follow his left hand. It is pointing to
the white awning of l'Auberge du Cheval Marin,
where one of the shoot-outs with *la Résistance* took
place. It was from here we witnessed *la Libération*.

me. I saw her at once. A black béret on her brown hair, she held a rifle. A dark leather jacket over her pleated skirt, running in short, sturdy boots; she appeared fearless.

Directly across the street, more gun smoke was visible from a round attic window above Maison Meurice's Wine Shop. This dramatic street scene startled neighbors in our building. Several stood on their balconies, watching, as we did, this rapid development taking place on our street, ten stories below. We continued passing the binoculars among us, since my father assured us we were safe.

This lasted five to ten minutes before the sniper's gunshots from the attic stopped. Minutes before, three men from la Résistance edged along the building, and entered through a low, service door. Now, only an eerie silence escaped from behind the dark, broken window. Their mission accomplished, the men dashed out and re-joined their determined camarades who now had reached the corner building, l'Auberge du Cheval Marin, from where the first gunman was still shooting. When a white flag appeared from the window, the Résistance fighters huddled together, nodded, and then signaled for the man to come down. One of the Résistance fighters, who was shot in the shoulder, sat on the sidewalk, propped against the building, while another leaned down and spoke to him. Still with the group, the woman had lost her béret. Her thick, brown hair was loose, she was beautiful, but seemed out of place surrounded by these tough men. Although, without her béret, she still firmly held her rifle.

Through an obscure, narrow doorway, a lone German soldier exited the building. Hesitant, his arms raised above his head, he bled profusely below his right shoulder. It was a horrible sight.

My grandmother murmured, "Ah, voila. Très bien, at least that poor soul will be returning to his family once this is all over. Ah, la, la, ah, oui. Mon Dieu, one less life lost in this awful war."

The Résistance group surrounded the frightened, wounded soldier and they headed back toward the park. But, since the gunshots had stopped, people ventured outside. Curious, vengeful, they surrounded the group with their German prisoner, taunting him, while closing their angry, menacing circle around him. A single shot rang out as he walked away, led by his captors. He fell to the ground, his cap still on his head, his arms were still raised as he lay flat on the dirt path near a bench.

Mamie gasped, her face flushed, "Ah, non! Mon Dieu, what a useless death! It will achieve nothing at this point, except another widow in the world will now weep." Sobbing, she ran to her bedroom.

We remained silent after that and, one by one, left our balcony. Papy turned his attention to the radio. Sitting in the corner chair, my father lit his pipe and read yesterday's newspaper. I followed my mother to the kitchen where we sang two of my favorite songs while we helped Juliette put things away. But my mother's voice kept breaking. She missed familiar words. Juliette was unusually quiet; her eyes were red and puffy. She blamed it on "peeling all those onions for tonight's onion soup."

The kitchen atmosphere was uncomfortable, so I decided to play in my room. Once alone, I wondered about the German soldier's wife. Who would go and tell her he had been killed? Would she ever be told how he died alone this afternoon far away, in a small park here in Brussels, instead of on a bloody battlefield? I wondered about his children. Would they wait for his return home? Believing that, one day he would re-appear, play ball with them as he used to? I thought about how he fell to the ground. Instantly. Never moving after his final moment in my favorite park.

The scent of tonight's onion soup drifted into my room. I now concentrated on braiding my doll's long, black hair. She needed a new hairdo.

Later that night, my grandparents stood over my bed. They disagreed. Mamie noted I was fast asleep and it was pointless to even try and wake me. Papy was insistent, gently calling out to me, "*Ma petite chérie*, wake up, come see, come on the balcony with us. *Les Alliés* have arrived!"

Minutes later, half-awake, I stood on our kitchen footstool, my coat over my pajamas, nestled between my grandparents. Together we waited under a clear, deep blue September sky and glistening stars, while from the railing our *beaux drapeaux* fluttered in a gentle evening breeze. In the streets below, people danced, waved small Belgian, British and American flags, shouting, "*Vive les Alliés! Vive la Libération! Vive la Belgique! Vive les Américains!*"

But the most unbelievable sight that night was right there on our familiar Rue de Flandre, when an endless convoy of tanks, jeeps, and open military trucks proceeded toward the center of Brussels, having just entered from the northern outskirts of the city. People threw flowers from their windows. Others ran along the sides of the moving convoy offering the soldiers bottles of cognac, wine, and Belgian beer. Girls, who managed to climb on some of the passing army vehicles, stood next to our weary, long-awaited heroes, who smiled and waved back to the delirious crowd.

A white banner, made from a sheet with crude red painted lettering, was strung from the balcony above Café Régina. It said: "*Vive les Alliés.*" On the opposite corner, at Café de Flandre, a loudspeaker was set-up. Music blared, from military marches, to popular accordion tunes. My grandparents called it, "*Un vrai pandémonium*" down below, and while I slept, my parents and Juliette went downstairs and were somewhere in the crowd celebrating *la Libération.*

The three of us stood a long time on our tenth-floor balcony, but as my grandmother began to weep, my grandfather tenderly hugged, then kissed her. Moments later he leaned down, took my hand and whispered, "Take a good look, *ma petite.* This evening, you are truly witnessing a page of history." He handed me his binoculars. While adjusting the strap, he declared, "*Oui*, always remember this evening. We have just been liberated!"

La Justice
September 1944

Two days after watching the Allies liberate us, I was playing in the bathtub, blowing soap bubbles aimed at the ceiling. From the kitchen, Mamie cautioned, "Only five more minutes *ma chérie!* It's time to get dressed. You're going with Juliette to Marché aux Poissons this morning."

My bath was now lukewarm. I replied, "*Oui*" and turned on more hot water. Seconds later I heard our front door open. It was Papy, returning with his morning newspaper. Instead of going to the salon and settling in his club chair, he rushed to the kitchen. Out of breath, he spoke in halted whispers. My grandmother gasped. Juliette's voice was hushed. Wrapped in a towel, I tip-toed to the bathroom door, opened it and tried to listen. The newspaper rustled. He read: "Citizens taking revenge against *les Boches.*" That didn't make sense; the Nazis fled Brussels two days ago. I saw them leave. His words spilled out so fast. I could not understand.

I gave up and stepped back into the soapy water

knowing my "five more minutes" were almost up. Juliette was agitated when she walked in then stepped in the puddle near the door. "*Ah, la, la,* what's this?" she exclaimed. "But, what a mess! What have you been doing in here?"

"Oh, nothing."

We headed to my room when the terrace door in the salon was opened. A burst of fresh air filled the hallway. My grandfather stepped outside with his binoculars and stared left toward my park. He called out, "Oh, Alice, it's true. It's really true. *Oh, Mon Dieu!*"

My grandmother spoke to Juliette, "Stay in here with *la petite* and keep this door closed." She joined him on the terrace.

I buttoned my jacket, ready to leave, when my grand-père appeared. "Juliette will go alone this morning and you'll stay here, *ma chérie.*"

Perfect. I never liked going to the nearby Marché aux Poissons with its noisy bustle, and carts delivering more fish, nearly bumping into the groups of busy shoppers. Almost a block long, the fish market was famous for its rows of open air stalls lined with tables of glistening fish displayed on mounds of crushed ice.

Its vendors bundled up against the cold; the women wearing rubber aprons and boots just like the men. Then there were the coarse, loud shouts as you passed by: "Very fresh sole, just caught this morning" or "*Alors, la belle,* let's go, fresh herring only ten *francs* a *kilog*" or "*Ah, oui,* Madame, *et bien,* how about a beautiful piece of haddock this morning?" At times, when hosing the ground around their stalls with cold water, the fishmongers inadvertently splashed our feet. The overpowering smell of raw fish was everywhere.

Juliette nodded, "Here, let's hang up your coat. I'll be back soon. Go play with your dolls." I obeyed, but it was not as interesting as whatever my grandparents had observed from our terrace this morning. When I asked Papy, he blurted out, "It was nothing. Nothing at all, ma chérie." Then he turned away.

When Juliette returned with the fish, she was hysterical. Her face flushed, she ran to the kitchen, sobbing into her hands. "Ah, Madame, Madame, it's true! It's true, I saw them!"

"But why, Juliette?" my grandmother whispered, "Why did you walk over to the park? You already knew."

"Oh, I don't know, Madame. I don't know. I was curious, and people at the marché were talking about it, so I followed a few of them to have a look, that's all. Oh, Madame, thank God, la petite stayed home."

Well, yes, she was right. I was relieved to stay home and play, but why had she returned crying? What was happening outside? In my park? This morning — My grandfather's newspaper. The answer was in his newspaper

I waited. And that afternoon, he left to do an errand. While Juliette ironed in the kitchen, and Mamie was in her bedroom writing her weekly letter to Aunt Yvonne in Rome, I sneaked to the salon. There, next to the radio, I found the folded morning paper. Soon I would know what the *fracas* of this morning was about. *Le mystère*. But, the newspaper rustled when unfolded, so I grabbed it and ran to the small bathroom, off the foyer. With the door locked, I flushed the toilet, opened the front page and saw them. Twisted bodies swinging from trees. I looked closer to understand.

They were German soldiers.

Shot.

Dead.

Hanging from tree branches in Brussels.

Then, I understood even more. In my favorite park next to our building. Yes, even there. Beneath the photos were words, "*Les Boches sont Finis.*" I flushed the toilet, folded the newspaper and ran water in the sink, while I sneaked out and replaced the folded newspaper near my grandfather's chair.

Juliette called out, "*Mais alors*, is everything all right in there?"

I turned off the water, "*Oh, oui.* I think I'd like to draw now," I replied in a low voice, "but I want to be in the kitchen with you."

"*Ah, oui !* That's nice. *Oui, alors*, come, *vite, vite, ma petite.*"

The following day, my parents and I went to visit my paternal grandparents. We rode the tram, but half-way along Avenue des Arts, several of the eight passengers murmured and gestured amongst themselves. Some stood, others switched to window seats next to the center of the Avenue, parallel to Boulevard du Régent across the way. I sensed something coming up. The tram slowed down. My mother stood and shielded my face against her body. "Don't look. *Oh, non, non, mon trésor. Non*, don't look!"

It was too late. I saw it, and I recalled the picture in the paper. The luxurious, olive drab, German car. Its impeccable, taut, canvas top, the deep, shiny, thick, leather seats. The windows were not rolled down but smashed. The powerful car had careened off the road, and due to the abrupt impact, was at an odd angle, a portion of its left fender embedded into one of the trees lining the avenue. A Nazi officer was slumped over the stirring wheel, his left arm dangling out. His mouth open. Blood had run from a bullet wound to his forehead and formed a dark circle on the ground. But, today the pool of blood was dry. Five or six passersby stood around the imposing automobile pointing and nodding, while from high above the sun's dappled light reached down through the leafy chestnut trees.

Our tram rolled on. Now, I knew death. I had just seen it. No longer a black and white photograph in the newspaper. It was real.

The passengers sat back down. Silence filled the tram. My mother whispered, "But, it's horrible. It's been two or three days."

My father replied, "*Oui*. It's *la justice.*"

A Black Truck
September 1944

By the third time I heard Juliette call my name, there was a growing annoyance in her voice. I picked up my doll, Suzette, as I wanted to take her with us this morning. While still buttoning her dress, I joined Juliette in the hallway, where she stood holding my blue jacket and our canvas grocery bag. "Hurry up. Let's go, *vite, vite.*" She locked our front door, and warned, "*Ah,* and today you'll have to carry Suzette by yourself. *Ah, mais oui,* by the time we've purchased all these things on your grand-mère's grocery list, there certainly won't be any room left in the bag for your doll." Once in the elevator, Juliette glanced at the list again and shook her head, "*Ah, la, la,* I wanted an earlier start this morning. Now that people are shopping again just like before the war, all the fresh, new items disappear immediately."

Instead of heading toward Sainte Catherine's outdoor market as usual, we practically ran in the opposite direction to a nearby *boulangerie.* Today was their grand re-opening. Juliette was not in a good mood this morning, so there was no conversation between us, which was perfectly fine with me, since I would have much preferred to stay in my room and serve tea to my dolls with the blue tea-set my grandfather brought me yesterday.

Even this early, the street was bustling with shoppers, wearing Belgian and Allied flag pins on their lapels. Our familiar Rue de Flandre was celebrating "*La Libération*" by wearing a new, colorful dress made from the large American, British and Belgian flags fluttering from windows and covering store-fronts, giving the street a joyful, festive feeling.

Since *la Libération* a week ago, people walked and behaved a lot more freely. My grandmother explained, "Fear and oppression has left along with the Germans. This new atmosphere in the streets reflects the relief and excitement at having survived the war, and of being freed." For me, it felt like waking from a long nightmare and just enjoying being still alive.

We neared the *boulangerie* when Juliette exclaimed, "Ah, *Zut!* Look at this queue. It's already eight o'clock. By the time it's our turn, the bread will be sold out. You were so slow. *Ah, oui,* and now, this is all your fault."

She was right; the line was long. Resigned, we stood at the end while early customers walked out proudly carrying their breads. A man shouted that *pistolets,* the popular round Belgian rolls, were once again sold inside.

When we finally reached the entrance, a boy, wearing

a baker's cap and an oversized white apron, made his way through the crowded shop while balancing a willow basket high above his head. His face, showing traces of flour, reminded me of a clown I saw once. He reached the front case, tipped the basket and hot *pistolets* tumbled upon the existing mounds, filling the window with an unfamiliar abundance. Their freshly baked, pale golden color was made even more startling next to the green tiles covering the outside of the *boulangerie*. I had never seen so much bread, and as I inhaled the pleasant, warm aroma, Juliette promised, "*Ah, oui* you'll see, *ma petite*. Tomorrow morning, you'll enjoy one of these crusty, *petits pistolets* for your breakfast. *Oh, oui*, they'll taste much better than our usual toast."

Once inside the narrow shop, I couldn't see anything because of my height. The moist aroma of freshly baked bread was overwhelming. I was surrounded by adults' large bodies, jammed against each other, their elbows and bulky satchels touching my face. Fearful of being crushed, I felt uneasy and needed more air. I pulled on Juliette's sleeve, and asked if I could wait outside. Reluctantly, she agreed. Holding Suzette close to me for her own protection, I wriggled across into the exiting line, and with relief, soon found myself back on the street breathing fresh air.

I stepped away from the crowded entrance, and peered into the shop window next door. It was filled with bolts of draped fabric, spools of ribbons, and velvet boards covered with buttons of every size, shape and color. I was trying to pick my favorites when people cleared the middle of the street while pointing and talking. A black truck was slowly heading toward me. It turned left into the short, narrow side street across the way and stopped. Four civilian men climbed down from the uncovered vehicle, then stood with menacing glares encircling it. I followed people gathering around the truck and soon, being small, I found myself in the front row. But, what I saw did not make sense.

Seven women were huddled together on the back of the truck. Frightened, they tried to turn their faces from the curious crowd. They were dressed in elegant dresses, unlike the drab, plain garments women normally wore. One was beautiful in a smooth cream satin dress. Their fancy hairstyles seemed unusual to me. After a wooden chair was placed in the middle of the flatbed truck by one of the men, he grabbed the first woman and ordered her to sit down. A large, cardboard sign with a red word painted on it, was hung around her neck. The crowd grew and was no longer curious, but angry. People shouted "Colla-Bo-Ra-Trices." What did it mean?

One of the men began cutting the long, brown, curly hair of the seated woman. It was odd, because it was not how Monique at Chez Antoine cut my hair. He grabbed and cut it too quickly. This man was not doing a good job. Then using a clipper, he shaved the rest completely off. The woman stared straight ahead. She looked awful. She looked like a boy, not a pretty girl. I felt embarrassed for her and knew she would not like seeing herself in the mirror later. The man made her stand alone and face the jeering crowd. People threw things and spat on her. Something hit her. It was a ripe tomato, which stained her soft blue, crepe flowered dress. It was only then she closed her eyes. I looked away and hugged Suzette tighter. I too closed my eyes. I did not feel very well.

When I looked again, a second woman, a blonde lady, was being shoved toward the chair. I caught her brief look of surprise at seeing me standing in the front row with my doll. The man also gave her an awful haircut, after placing a cardboard sign around her neck. But this time, as he began shaving her head and the last of her soft blond curls fell around her, he shouted things in Flemish. The crowd laughed. It was an ugly, mean laughter. People who lived on this street opened their windows, and from the second and third stories, threw garbage, aiming it at the pretty ladies. Surrounded by people, stunned, yet spellbound, I watched.

From the back of the crowd, Juliette shouted my name. I called her name back, and we found each other. After crossing herself, shielding my eyes with our canvas bag, she yanked me away by the arm, babbling over and over, "Oh, *ma petite, non! Oh, non, Mon Dieu!*" Once across the street she knelt down while scolding me and with trembling fingers, adjusted one of my hair ribbons which had come undone. Abruptly, she stopped, and instead, with teary eyes, she began to kiss and hug me. She dabbed her eyes and blurted, "Ah, *ma petite, ma petite. Ah,* thank God,"

Her eyes were still teary as hand-in-hand, we finally

headed to the outdoor market. She tore a warm piece of bread and handed it to me and I confided, "I'm so happy you found me. It was just the right time too, because I don't like what I've been watching alone over there."

Juliette was so relieved to have found me, she even agreed Suzette needed a nap, and placed her in our canvas bag, next to the loaf of bread and the *pistolets*, as now, for some reason, my doll felt too heavy. We walked in silence until we stopped to buy fruits from a street cart.

"But, Juliette, tell me why? Why did the ladies allow their hair to be cut this way, and — even shaved? And why in front of those people?" Juliette did not reply but made her selection. "What is 'Collab – calabatriss' anyway? What does it mean?"

She ignored me and placed her purchase in our canvas bag. But, moments later, once we resumed our walk she stammered, in a low voice, "Ah, well, you see *ma petite*, these were pretty, but, well . . . very naughty ladies, who were . . . friends with the Nazis, and today were punished for their mistake. People are quite angry and . . . to punish them, made them look ugly, but only for a while . . . naturally. That's it *petite. Voila.* That's all."

"Will their pretty curls ever grow back?"

Too quickly, she blurted out, "Ah, *oui*, but of course, *ma petite. Oui*, very soon."

We had just reached Sainte Catherine's market. "But why? Why didn't they just all go together to Chez Antoine?"

This time, Juliette never answered. Instead, she handed me another piece of bread. It was still warm.

Post Cards from The Tate
October 1944 – April 1946

The unmistakable rustle of Sister Evangeline's long, black skirt, brought me back to reality. I stopped drawing, but it was too late. Her flushed, angry face hovered over me. She snatched my notebook and held it high. Loud snickers from first graders resonated in the classroom.

Lost in my day dreams, I had ignored her assignment, drawing instead pine trees in my notebook. Sister Evangeline marched me to the front of the class. With a ruler kept inside her desk, she whacked my outstretched hands, and concentrated the ten blows upon my small, extended, fingers. My thirty classmates, looked on, curious and amused.

"Go stand in the corner, and face the wall." She placed the cardboard cone on my head. I became the class dunce. Laughter filled the classroom until the lesson resumed, to be interrupted with occasional muffled snickers throughout the morning period.

Mortified, I stood alone in the corner crying. I wanted

to disappear. But for this I needed a miracle. Anything. I stared down at the floorboards. If only they could part, it would allow me to vanish beneath the classroom until lunchtime. If that didn't work, and I prayed hard enough, I could, perhaps, get some other type of Divine help — to just evaporate right through the ceiling and disappear into the sky. Float away above the school. Sister Evangeline would really be sorry then, but it would be too late. I might wave down to her. Maybe not. Eyes closed tight, I began to pray.

After praying hard for a few minutes, I opened my eyes to find myself still in the corner. I noticed King Léopold staring at me from his place of honor on the wall. The war now over, his portrait was back, once again hanging in all classrooms. Dressed in his beige military uniform, he had returned to observe our scholastic progress in silence.

Ah, oui, and there was the proof, our daily prayers with brave Sister Maria were heard up in heaven. What a difference from last year, when a flushed Mother Superior, her black serge habit rustling, rushed in, and interrupted our kindergarten class. Distraught, she warned, "Ah, please *mes enfants,* we must all prepare. We have been notified that German Commandants can march into our classrooms for inspection at any time. The portrait of Adolph Hitler must be displayed on the wall at once. No further mention or picture of our King is allowed, or severe retribution will occur." This announcement was met with murmured boos from the boys and nervous squeals and cringing from the girls.

Yet, from that day on, every morning before class began, Sister Maria took King Léopold's portrait out of hiding, propped it on her desk and led us in a short prayer for his health and safety. As we stood next to our desks in our short blue smocks, in unison we prayed aloud. Frightened, I listened for sounds of heavy German boots marching in the corridor. Filled with dread, I wondered what the Nazi commandant would do to us for breaking rules. I sensed it would be an immediate punishment. They might put us in a green truck, and take us away, like Marcel.

So, my kindergarten year was spent in a classroom observed by the sharp, beady black eyes of a bareheaded Adolph Hitler in his Nazi uniform.

But all that was before *la Libération*, and today, King Léopold's portrait was back in its place of honor. As I stared up, I wondered if he could see me and, more important, if back at his palace he would soon be informed of my misbehavior by Mother Superior.

The lunch bell rang, Sister Evangeline dismissed the class. Free to go home, I lingered behind, listened, to make sure my classmates left before I ventured to the cloakroom, to avoid the danger of more ridicule. Since it was lunch time, the narrow Rue Rempart des Moines, with its constricted dank *ruelles*, alleys, was deserted. But running while crying is a difficult thing. I tried to button my coat, but my fingers were bruised! I missed the first button. My coat hung lopsided. Across Rue Antoine Dansaert, I ran on the cobblestones, passed surprised pedestrians until, ten minutes later, I reached up and rang our door bell. Juliette, wiping her hands on her apron, opened the door. I rushed passed her to the bathroom.

"Hurry up, *vite, vite,* that's right. *Oui,* wash your hands. *Le déjeumer* is ready. We're having your favorite noodles." I held my hands under cold water. It soothed the pain. I splashed cold water over my face and combed my bangs, but nothing worked. My face was still red.

From the kitchen Juliette shouted, "*Alors,* how was school this morning? I missed you. Guess what we're having for dessert today? Flan. So, *vite, vite,* come and help me set the table." I straightened my school uniform and ventured to the dining room to finish setting the table with the silverware she laid on the table corner.

I kissed my grandparents, "*Bonjour*" but both were distracted; discussing the radio program they just heard. Plates were served. The bread was passed, Papy gasped, "Ah, but, *ma chérie,* what's happened to your hands?" I hid them under the table. "And why were you crying?"

Juliette sitting next to me gently placed my hands back on the table. The red marks had darkened, my fingers were stiff. "So, *petite,* it is important you tell us *exactement,* what happened at school this morning." But I remained silent.

My grand-mère insisted, "*Mais oui,* how did this happen to your fingers? Explain, if you please."

Finally, I mumbled, "I guess, I did not pay attention and Sister Evangeline punished me." The real problem was my classmates spoke only Flemish. I did not. Feeling apart from them, I chose day-dreaming and drawing in my notebook.

My grandfather was angry. "Ah, *quelles vaches! Ah, non.* That is far too much!"

Lunch continued. Mamie shook her head once or twice in silence until Juliette served the flan. "*Oh*, I have an errand to do this afternoon. I am picking up an English book I ordered weeks ago, and I would like you to join me. *Oui, petite*, you'll come with me, *et voila.*"

Papy added, "*Ma chère* Alice, *oui, quelle bonne idée. Oui, absolument.* You both have a nice afternoon. In fact, I, too, have an errand. Something I have to take care of *immédiatement.*"

The five story Old England Department Store was located in an Art Nouveau building across Brussels on Rue de Caudenberg, but this branch, the three-storied Old England Bookstore, was nearby on Boulevard Adolphe Max. I enjoyed entering this stately, old British store, walking on its highly polished, inlaid wooden floors. I inhaled the scent of freshly printed paper and ink escaping from books on wooden racks. They lined the walls and aisles, offering collections of English books and countless British magazines and newspapers. The elevator, with red carpet and ornate, polished brass, grilled doors, was run by a man in a red suit with gold buttons and a red cap. If I asked permission, we would ride up and down twice. And today, we did. Once my grandmother's long-awaited book was wrapped in the store's green monogrammed paper, we rode the lift to the third-floor tea-room.

Closed during the war, this oasis, the glass-domed tea-room, had just re-opened. We sat at one of the small tables covered with a starched white tablecloth. From this third-floor gallery, enclosed by walls lined with more books hidden by potted palms and the scrolled bronze balustrade, I could see the shop's clientele moving on both levels below. When we were served our tea and English scones, I once again hid my hands beneath the tablecloth.

Before leaving, we stopped by the wooden stand filled with postcards of famous paintings from the Tate Museum in London. I was allowed to choose a favorite for my card collection, and was close to my final decision, when my grandmother suggested, "Why don't you choose a second one? They are so beautiful. The choice is really quite difficult."

I selected, "Crossing the Brook," which reminded me of Parc de la Cambre and its mysterious wooded island, and "Venice, the Bridge of Sighs," because I liked Venice's canals with all those boats and colorful flags everywhere. Except for the sharp pain in my fingers, our afternoon together helped me forget this morning. Returning home, we were both pleased. Mamie held her beautifully wrapped book; I carried my postcards in a green, monogrammed Old England envelope. During our walk, with great delight, she told me about the numerous travels of Monsieur Turner whose paintings on the rack had caught my fancy. He visited Belgium, admired the city of Bruges and sketched its canals.

The next morning, during my breakfast with Juliette,

she said, "Oh, you will not be leaving for school as usual today. After you're dressed, your grandparents wish to see you in the salon." I dressed quickly and minutes later, sat on the plum settee next to Mamie.

Papy stood and announced, "With only four weeks left before the school year ends, a decision has been made. Since *la Libération*, it is no longer necessary for you to attend the nearest school. Your days at Rue T'Kint Catholic Primary are over."

Mamie added, "*Oui précisément*. Now that the war has ended, the danger of bombing is gone. In the fall, you will be enrolled at another school, Rue du Marais, with perhaps a longer walking distance. *Ah*, and of course, *ma petite*, classes there are in French."

It took a few moments for the news to sink in. Elated, I hugged them both. "Oh, but, tell me, do they wear uniforms?"

With a smile, Mamie replied, "*Ah, non*. No more uniforms."

I could hardly believe my good fortune. A miracle! My prayers were answered.

La Victoire
June 1945

On a Sunday morning, at the age of six, I watched as my parents separated. Not only controlling, my father was also prone to angry moods, best described by my grandfather as, "A somber, ill-tempered storm seems to come over him."

Because, my father always disapproved of whatever I did, I had learned to stay away as best I could, and since he showed very little interest in me, it was the perfect solution for both of us. My mother constantly wept into her lace handkerchiefs, but when friends questioned her red eyes, she replied, "Oh, it is just a little head cold. Nothing serious."

Juliette was appalled and often consoled her, "Ah, my *pauvre* Madame, *ah, la, la,* please don't cry anymore. *Voila, voila* here's another handkerchief." Or, "Ah, *la, la,* Monsieur appears to be in one of his dark moods today, but don't worry, Madame, God will punish him. Ah, *oui,* Madame, one day you'll see."

The last time I saw my father and mother together in

My train set, a favorite toy — and a diversion.

their apartment was that Sunday morning in June, I was playing on the floor of the salon with my train set as he exited our lives.

He never kissed me goodbye, but did say "My recently-purchased console radio will be picked up at a later date." Pointing to my mother, he warned, "And you, are *absolument* forbidden to touch it. This radio is mine. Only I alone can touch it." And with a stern, determined look upon his face, carrying his suitcases out he went, slamming the door behind him.

My mother collapsed on the blue ottoman, weeping. Immediately, Juliette came from the kitchen, still drying a plate with her red and white checkered *torchon*. She knelt at my mother's side, and began consoling her.

After a few minutes, and my mother's use of several handkerchiefs, Juliette stood, shook her head and declared, "Ah, *la, la* Monsieur was very mean not to allow you, Madame, to listen to his new radio."

My mother sniffled, "Ah, *oui*, unfortunately Juliette, this is so true."

They recalled, how only yesterday, the music was so lovely. They even hummed bits of a song, and agreed what a shame this pleasure was now forbidden.

Moments passed while they both reflected upon the current situation.

"But since Monsieur is gone," whispered Juliette, "Why doesn't Madame enjoy some music? It would definitely bring a little *gaieté* to the apartment on such a sad day." My mother dabbed her eyes with another fresh handkerchief, pondered upon Juliette's words, and seconds later, decided it made sense.

As both stood side-by-side in front of the gleaming new radio, my mother found the "on" knob and turned it. *Rien.* Nothing. No lights. No sound. *Silence.* This was fascinating. Where indeed was the music? Both women became upset. Juliette stomped her foot. My mother, her face flushed, furiously pushed and turned every button. Nothing. Not even a tiny squeak from the large box.

They tilted it slightly to see if, perhaps, another switch was hidden under it. They had just given up, when Juliette dropped to her knees, wriggled behind the wood console, and reached for the cord. "*Ah,* but, Madame, look — he has disconnected it!" Brandishing the unplugged cord as evidence, she re-appeared, slightly disheveled, from behind the heavy cabinet.

My mother gasped, "*Oh, Mon Dieu,* my God, what a horrible and cruel thing to do! Let's plug it back in *immédiatement.*" It took only a moment for them to move it aside. Juliette then re-plugged the radio. At once it spurted, crackled, sent strange high-pitched whistling sounds as its hypnotizing, round emerald green light re-appeared on the black glass panel.

"*La victoire!*" exclaimed my mother. After she made a few adjustments of various knobs, the radio offered us a cheerful love song, *Boom!* by the popular French singer Charles Trénet. A fragment of this *chanson d'amour* said, "And when our heart goes Boom, Boom!" To my surprise and delight, with each refrain my mother and Juliette, standing close together, sang the words "Boom, Boom!" in unison.

From that magic moment, happiness filled the salon. My mother smiled, Juliette danced, twirling her kitchen *torchon*. Fascinated by this transformation, I realized a dark spell had just been broken.

We spent that Sunday afternoon listening to the latest French songs performed by Damia, Edith Piaf, and my mother's favorite, the dark, suave, Corsican sensation, Tino Rossi, surnamed "The Napoleon of Romance", and many others.

Late in the afternoon, my mother sent Juliette to the corner *patisserie* for ice cream with our three favorite flavors, mocha, raspberry and chocolate written on a piece of paper, as Juliette could sometimes be forgetful.

The gravelly voice of another Edith Piaf's lamenting love song, *Mon Légionnaire* drifted to the terrace where we stood together and even shared our ice creams. After an eventful, stormy morning, we enjoyed a rare joyful, memorable afternoon, and my mother smiled.

I had not seen that in a long time.

On the Boulevard
October 1945

After the Liberation, and the grim, menacing Nazis had gone, the city of Brussels changed. It was now a vibrant, different city, her boulevards bustling with Allied soldiers in various uniforms. Usually walking in groups of three to five, sometimes with arms linked, they sang, *When Johnny Comes Marching Home* or *It's a Long Way to Tipperary* and *We're Going to Hang our Clothes on the Siegfried Line*. These were American and British sailors, paratroopers, airmen, and soldiers. The ladies in uniform were called WACS and WAVES and wore tight, uncomfortable, military suits with neckties. Their hats, barely resting on their coiffed, permed hair, offered the constant possibility of sliding away.

The Allies were friendly, generous in sharing their tins of corned beef, cigarettes, oranges, chocolate bars, and a strange item called, "*le choo-ing gomme.*" Belgians took to "*choo-ing gomme,*" for not only was it something new, but it made them feel more closely connected to the Allies if they also chewed some *gomme* while walking down the street. It was a forbidden thing at our house. After my grand-mère stated, "Ah, *non*. After all, so far, we are not yet like cows, chewing cud!" Juliette tried it once in secret, on our way to the market, but she didn't like it and got rid of it. While walking home, she complained,

"Oh, *la*, *la*, and now after all that constant chewing, my jaw hurts, and worse yet, now I feel hungry."

Charles de Gaulle and Lord Bernard Montgomery, nicknamed "Monty", came to Brussels to receive our "Thank you" for liberating us. A month later, Winston Churchill came as well, and I saw them all with my mother and grandparents at La Grand' Place.

Often in the afternoons, my grandfather and I sat together, at his desk and prepared an important chart to help us identify the nationality and branch of the armed services of the Allied servicemen we passed on the street. While we worked together, he explained the bravery of the Allies who crossed the Atlantic, to free us from the Nazis and added. "Never forget *ma chérie*, thousands of Americans have given their lives on Normandy beaches to save us." He described how the daring, American paratroopers landed in total darkness in the Ardennes, and the deadly Battle of the Bulge. I was allowed to glue the two miniature paper flags, an American flag and a British. Below, separated by red pencil lines, each branch of the armed services was listed in separate columns. We had fun, listing our descriptions and comments

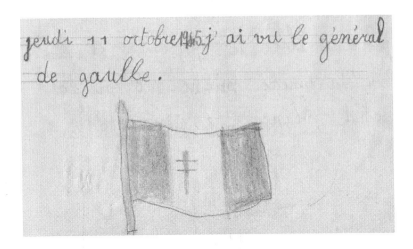

jeudi 11 octobre 1945 j' ai vu le général de gaulle.

An important date in *"Cahier de Souvenirs à Françoise"* — my souvenir notebook. The flag is the Free French Flag, which was flown during the war. It is the *tricolores*: blue, white and red, with the red Croix de Lorraine, the symbol of Joan of Arc.

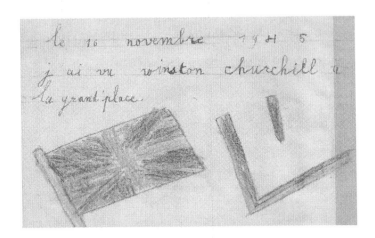

le 16 novembre 1945 j' ai vu winston churchill à la grand place.

Another important entry. Please note Churchill's cigar and the "V for Victory!", along with the British flag.

of different uniforms, often adding our detailed drawings, which we glued on the back. He often reminded me, "This chart we're working on, *ma petite*, is a rare one. This is what they call, A Significant Historical Chart. *Oui. Absolument.* It's true, *ma chérie!*"

On this sunny, September afternoon, returning home from an errand, rather than walking on cobblestone streets, my grandmother suggested, "Why don't we turn here instead, *ma petite*, and enjoy the new sights along Boulevard Adolphe Max?"

"Oh, *oui*. What a great idea! *Oui*, let's go."

Shops closed during the war were re-opening and store fronts with new awnings, their windows draped with Belgian, French and Allied flags, gave an exuberant feel to the previously somber, grey boulevard. On this balmy, September afternoon, passersby displayed with pride their newly purchased American and British flag pins on their lapels. They appeared carefree, swept up by this still unfamiliar, joyful atmosphere. Women dressed in more colorful, chic clothing, walked differently, their heads held high. The men appeared slightly dapper, some wearing a carnation in their lapels, or colorful handkerchiefs in their breast pockets.

Sidewalk cafés were crowded with Allied troops, busy sampling the famous Belgian beers, enjoying well-deserved leaves. Whenever we passed these noisy, crowded cafés, I avoided the pungent smell of beer mixed with heavy, thick tobacco smoke by quickly holding my breath. But, when fragments of English or American songs drifted outside, I slowed down to see and hear more, until I was led away. Sometimes, inside larger crowded, smoke-filled cafés, two or three separate groups of servicemen often with arms linked, gathered around a table to sing their favorite, ignoring others singing different songs.

Basking in this unfamiliar, festive atmosphere, we strolled past a new shop. Customers seemed pleased as they left, enjoying their ice cream cones. Others, holding tall paper cups with straws, were busy sipping the new American invention called the "*Le Milk-Shake*."

"Ah, *oui*, look, *ma chérie*, this shop looks inviting. *Oui*, of course. . . Ah, and look at that sign. But, I wonder— What exactly do you think is *Le Milk-Shake d'Amérique?*"

"I don't know, but perhaps we should go inside and try their ice cream?"

Curious, we entered the white-tiled shop. A glass-front counter, the length of the shop, separated the queue of waiting customers from rows of cardboard cylinders filled with different, colorful, ice cream. With so many flavors to choose from, my final decision was going to be difficult. Mamie began reading the list of flavors offered on the overhead board. But as she was describing a Milk-Shake, three handsome American soldiers entered the shop, walked to the front of the line, and the first one, speaking in English, demanded immediate service. What amazed me was that he was the most muscular man I had ever seen, and he was black. Dressed in their intriguing, camouflage uniforms, complete with puttees and sturdy, laced-up, leather combat boots, I recognized the insignia and their bérets: Paratroopers. Dazzled by them, I forgot about ice-cream flavors.

At once, I knew these were true, magnificent, fearless warriors, not just soldiers. These American paratroopers exuded an unusual, slightly arrogant, lithe, powerful strength, so different from the somber, demeanor of the rigid menacing, Nazi soldiers.

I stared at all three, but remained fascinated by the imposing black paratrooper who, speaking English, apparently told the petite, blonde Flemish woman behind the counter what they wanted, and wanted now. Waiting customers, surprised by their abrupt entrance, stepped aside and allowed the paratroopers to go first. But the woman ignored them. She took the order of the person behind them, and muttered something to which a few people nodded in agreement. This infuriated the paratrooper. Pointing at a picture of a Milk-Shake up on the board, he shouted something at the woman who continued to ignore him while scooping out more ice cream.

Tension mounted in the narrow, crowded shop.

My grandmother, who spoke English, leaned down and whispered, "*Alors*, just stay in line, *ma petite*. Don't move." She walked up to the counter, gave a formal nod to the paratroopers. Then, standing next to them, said to the woman in French, "Why don't you just give them what they'd like so we can all get on with our orders?"

But the woman, busy scooping out ice cream, shook her head and replied, "Ah, *mais* Madame, so many of these Allied soldiers come here almost every day and expect it for free. They never want to pay. I have to make a living after all, especially after this stinking war."

There was a low rumbling in the waiting crowd. Customers sympathized with the woman, until my grandmother declared in her distinct, firm voice, "Ah, but *ma chère* Madame, we would still be in the middle of your 'stinking war' if it weren't for the Allies and these brave men. Instead of complaining, you should be proud to serve them any ice cream flavor they wish, every day if necessary, and, *absolument, toujours* for free!"

At once, a noticeable change took place. People murmured, "Ah *oui*, it's quite true. Well said, Madame." This, as several customers, shook their heads in disapproval, left the line and walked out. Surprised, then embarrassed, the woman, her face flushed with anger, reluctantly turned to the three soldiers and filled their orders in silence. Pleased, the paratroopers took the first sip of their frothy Milk-Shakes.

In unison, the three fearless, magnificent American paratroopers saluted their silent "thank you" to my grandmother. Smiling, each holding their Milk-Shakes, they exited the shop, and with great bravado, stepped into the glorious September afternoon on the boulevard. Embarrassed, yet proud of my grandmother's courage, I was relieved when, returning to my side, she asked, "So, what would you prefer this afternoon, *ma chérie,* raspberry or pistachio?"

Holding on to her arm, my face pressed against her, I whispered, "Pistachio, please."

The Red Belt
July-August 1946

Every Sunday, beginning two months after my parents separated, I was sent to spend the day with my paternal grandparents. I resented these obligatory visits, but this weekly ordeal seemed to be an unbreakable law.

My father, always smoking, waited for me at the tram stop near his parent's apartment building. Dressed in a somber color, double-breasted jacket, dark grey trousers and immaculate white shirts, he seemed nervous and angry. He probably did not want to go there either. After the formal *"Bonjour, Papa"* followed by a proper kiss on the cheek, we crossed Avenue Marnix, to sit at the corner café, beneath one of several, red umbrellas. This was different for me, as my family never went to cafés. However, on Sundays, everything now seemed *à l'envers* anyway. He ordered a glass of Sandeman Port, sometimes two, and a pink grenadine for me. Once fortified, he led me to the twelfth-floor penthouse to both be greeted with a reserved and a cool welcome from his parents.

These Sunday visits were tedious. I was not allowed to speak during the long formal dinner. Afterward, I was expected to play quietly with two or three toys kept in the bottom of the kitchen cupboard, or to sit and read alongside my grandmother in her sunny, blue boudoir at the far end of the apartment. She favored mystery novels and always remained engrossed in her book. From a box of chocolates on the table beside her blue velvet divan, I was allowed to select two, sometimes three, chocolates. With little conversation between us, I resigned myself to these long, monotonous, Sunday afternoons.

A year later, I was now seven, on a Sunday in July, things changed. After the usual Sunday dinner, my father announced, "We will be leaving early today." Minutes later, back on Avenue Marnix, we walked in silence until we reached Avenue de la Toison d'Or.

"Papa, why can't we just take the tram back home?"

"You'll see. There is an errand we must do first." I was puzzled. Errands were done in various stores, but today was Sunday. All stores were closed. After a few minutes I voiced my concern.

"But, Papa, are we walking such a long distance, perhaps in vain"?

"We are going to my new apartment," and led us off the avenue to a short, narrow, sunless side street. But what was this mysterious errand?

He unlocked a heavy black forged iron and glass front

door to a grey stone, four-storied apartment building. Once inside, I followed him along a dark hallway. Our footsteps echoed on the black marble floor, but the lack of sounds from behind any apartment doors we passed left me uneasy. In front of the last door, he stopped. "Just wait outside." He turned the key and went inside. I heard a woman's soft voice, and light girlish laughter. Suddenly, the door re-opened and they both came out.

Introductions took place in the dark hallway. Her name was Yvette. She kissed me, touched the top of my head, and admired my long hair, as my father locked his apartment door. The three of us stepped outside in the warm, summer Sunday afternoon. But, who was she? And, why was she left alone in my father's apartment?

Once in the sunlight, I noticed Yvette was young and pretty. Sandy, fluffy hair framed her face. She wore bright red lipstick and was dressed all in white, except for a wide, red leather belt. Looking down, I admired her shiny, very high, red heels.

We walked a long way. My father and Yvette chatted. She wore dainty, white summer gloves, giggled a lot and, a rare thing, she made my father smile. Soon, she switched places with me and I held both fathers' and Yvette's hands. My father seemed different with Yvette than he had been with my mother, an interesting change for the better, of course. Finally, we boarded a tram at La Porte de Hal, a museum famous for its collection of arms and armor as Yvette's new red shoes had given her blisters.

The next Sundays were the same, except now, after Sunday dinner, Yvette met us on the tree-lined Avenue de la Toison d'Or, where my father bought us ice cream from a stand. The three of us sat on a park bench. Giggling, Yvette announced, in a deep voice, "And now, let us savor our delicious ice cream." For the first time, she made the Sundays spent with my father enjoyable, and for this, I liked her. She was great. I loved her dresses, always white, wearing the same red belt, and, of course, her shiny, high-heeled red shoes. I told her how pretty she was, how happy the three of us were during these Sunday afternoons, and of the change in my father. And for that I squeezed her hand in gratitude.

A few Sundays later, my father announced, "Today we are invited to *chez* Yvette." I liked that. I enjoyed visiting people's homes, looking out their windows, inspecting their favorite small trinkets, knowing I would be rewarded with sweets during the visit.

Soon we arrived in front of a small, three-story apartment house on a sunny street, where houses looked similar, neat and nondescript. My father pushed her doorbell. We waited on the sidewalk for the buzzer to sound, allowing us entry into the building. He rang three times, but there was only silence. No response. With apprehension, I suggested to my father, "Perhaps you have the wrong house number?" Just then, the buzzer sounded, allowing us entry into an immaculate, small hallway that smelled of soap and freshly waxed floors. We climbed a polished, narrow staircase to the second-floor landing. A man was just leaving. He barely looked at us and rapidly descended the stairs.

Yvette stood in front of her opened door and smiled. She must have just washed her hair. It seemed to bounce around her face more than usual. I was surprised, she was still in a pretty rose satin-flowered robe. She seemed happy to see us. I handed her the bouquet of feathery ferns and delicate pink roses my father and I just bought from a corner vendor on the boulevard. She arranged them in a vase, placed it on the coffee table, then served us some refreshments, including something new and different, chocolate covered almonds. She seemed a little nervous, when she handed my father a package of cookies from her kitchen cupboard, then asked him for help in opening it. "These are only for you," she said to me with a wink. She gave me a tour of her small apartment, and introduced me to her little canary, Chéri, kept in a cage by the window.

Yvette's apartment was bright and spotless. The parquet floor was buffed to a glossy shine. A beige sofa with a bright red rug in front of it took up most of the living room. With a rattan coffee table, and two matching chairs with red floral cushions, there was little room to move around. A wooden door with rectangular, frosted-glass panels, separated the living room from the rest of the apartment, a tiny square hallway with three doors leading to the bedroom, a small bathroom, and the minimal kitchen. Having concluded the tour of her apartment, Yvette placed a pad of writing paper and some pencils on the coffee table. "I know how much you like to draw, so these are all for you." She brought a stack of fashion magazines, "There, you can study these. Pick your favorite dresses for when you grow up. There are some very beautiful things."

My father had disappeared when Yvette gave me strict instructions, "First, you should be *très sage,* very good. Finish all the cookies if you like. Look at the pretty pictures in the magazines and draw whatever you want. We will be out in a while after we have a serious discussion. Then the three of us will go out for our Sunday promenade and ice cream, as always." What could I do? It seems I was stuck in Yvette's living room. I was a little disappointed. She made me promise, "Under no circumstances, should you open the door to anyone. Absolutely no one. Most important of all, do not ever push the buzzer to the downstairs front door." She then made me swear to all this, after which she said, "Be a good girl." After I used the bathroom, she closed the frosted glass-paneled door behind her. I heard a key being turned and the click of the lock. Suddenly, I was alone.

Très bien, just me and the yellow canary. After a few minutes, the novelty of seeing the small bird flutter back and forth as I moved the branch of thistle in the cage lost its appeal. I pushed aside the draperies and looked down at the small, cheerless, garden below. I then studied the four, stylized jungle prints in black frames hanging above a black chest of drawers but Yvette's apartment was boring. Except for Chéri the canary, she had no small objects for me to look at. I glanced at a few fashion magazines, but soon turned my attention to the pencils and pad of paper. After testing several of the pencils, I picked the one I liked best.

I placed the two chair cushions on the floor next to the coffee table. Seated comfortably I began to draw.

Someone rang the bell downstairs. Incessantly. Its persistent shrillness scared me. Who could it be? Was it some emergency? I felt confused. What should I do? I walked toward the buzzer, but remembered my promise to Yvette. The ringing continued, but I did exactly what Yvette asked and sat very still on the sofa, hoping whoever it was, would go away and come back later. The ringing stopped. I heard a buzzer from another apartment, then heavy footsteps coming up the stairs. I thought whoever it was had gone away, but now someone was outside the apartment door, ringing the bell. I covered my ears. What a situation! The sound of a firm knock added to my fear. There was no place for me to hide. From behind the door a man's voice said, "Yvette, open the door, I have some presents for you."

Well, that changed everything. Yvette would like presents. Standing on my toes I reached up and unlocked the door. Immediately, I regretted having done so. A gruff, tall man, dressed in an American Army officer's uniform and carrying boxes, took two steps into the tiny living room, pushing me aside. In an American accent he inquired, "Are you totally deaf? I've been standing outside on the street below with my gifts for Yvette, trying to come up and see her." Abruptly, he stopped: "Who are you anyway? What are you doing here?"

"I am a guest of Yvette and am just waiting for them to come out, so we can go for our Sunday promenade and ice cream."

He leaned down, "Who did you come with, then?"

"Why, mon Papa," I replied, "He's inside with Yvette. They locked the door because they are having a serious discussion."

The officer's face reddened. He grabbed his presents shouted, "Hell!" and rushed out, slamming the door behind him.

This afternoon was definitely not going as planned. We should be out, having fun. A key turned, the door opened, and Yvette and my father re-appeared in the living-room. Dressed in a white dress, she wore her customary red belt and shoes. I was scolded for opening the door and breaking my promise. I explained, "But Yvette, he brought you some presents, and I thought at the time, you would like that."

"So, where are they?" she asked.

"Well — He seemed a little angry. Then he just left. And, that's when he took all your presents away . . . in two cartons."

Yvette smiled. "Let us go for our Sunday walk then, as always." We had a nice time that afternoon, even with a late start.

That evening, back in the tenth-floor nest, during supper, I asked, "Maman, why do you always dress so serious? Perhaps you should buy yourself a red belt just like Yvette's and — why not? Bright red shoes, too."

"Who is Yvette?" my mother asked, surprised.

"But, just how did you meet Yvette, *ma chérie?*" my grandmother inquired.

"*Oui, ma petite*, please tell us — who is this Yvette?" my grandfather insisted on knowing.

Within a few minutes of my detailed explanation, my mother placed a call to my paternal grandparents and informed them of just how my father and I had been spending our Sunday afternoons, explaining our mysterious departures immediately after dinner. That was the *la finale* of those, happy Sundays.

Years later, I figured out Yvette's source of income. But, I still liked her, for during those few summer Sundays she made the time spent with my father a lot more pleasant.

Nadine
October 1946 - May 1947

That September, I was enrolled at my paternal grandmother's alma mater, *Lycée Gatti de Gamond,* Rue du Marais, where I experienced a new freedom. The *Lycée* conducted their classes in French. Here I explored new subjects, including geography and Belgian history. Best of all, as promised, there were no uniforms. My classmates accepted me although I was different. I didn't speak Flemish.

One mid-morning in October, Madame la Directrice entered our second-grade classroom with a new student, Nadine. She was pale, shy and tiny. So small, I wondered whether Madame had made a mistake, bringing her to our second-grade classroom. Nadine was assigned the desk next to mine. She did not smile, but carefully placed her notebooks and pencil kit in her desk, then sat straight up, clasped her hands together and stared ahead. Class resumed.

Nadine did not mingle with us at recess. She stood alone against a wall or walked around the walled-in school yard

Lycée Royal-Gatti de Gamond, my school.

Proof that I studied well.

and watched us play ball or tag. After a few weeks, we stopped asking her to join us and ignored her. Apparently, it was what she wanted, and seemed more comfortable that way.

Her mother braided her long, blonde hair in several thin braids at the front, then gathered them in a long, thick, silken braid, which hung down her frail back. I was envious. My two braids were basic and severe, hair parted in the middle, one braid on each side with plaid ribbons at the end. Sometimes they were pinned up like a crown on top of my head. I asked Juliette, "Oh, please tell me how long will it take for my hair to grow down to the middle of my back, to have a braid as long as Nadine's?"

"Oh, but long hair like that is not for you. *Oh non. Non.* Besides you wouldn't like it. It's not practical and tangles all up when you shampoo it. We both know how you hate snarls."

Nadine excelled in grammar and geography. She memorized her multiplication tables and when our teacher, Madame Oudenne asked us questions, Nadine was usually the first to raise her hand.

Her schoolbag was too large for her. Because of its weight, she leaned to one side when going down the curved, steep stairwell after classes. Due to my own unhappy experiences last year, I wanted Nadine to be happier. I smiled constantly at her, until one day she smiled back. Soon, she began to laugh when we did and one day she joined us and played tag. She could not run fast. Her legs were weak, and she fell twice.

There were no classes on Thursday afternoons and I asked permission to invite Nadine to our home. My grandparents agreed. But, when I asked for her telephone number Nadine replied, "Ah, *non, c'est impossible*. We don't have a telephone."

She had once confided that her father was a *chapelier*, a hat maker, and that his shop was across the street from the renowned Le Saint-Sauveur Indoor Pool. My grandfather suggested that on the way home from school that afternoon we could detour by her father's shop and he would speak to her parents. It was a longer walk, but I looked forward to seeing Nadine.

We reached Rue Montagne aux Herbes Potagères and looked for a *chapelier*. The hat shop was so dimly lit and non-descript, we passed by it and had to retrace our steps twice. Side-by-side, we finally stood in front of its narrow, meager display window. In there were three men's felt hats on mannequin heads. A pearl-grey fedora with a black grosgrain ribbon, set between two black hats. Three wool caps were displayed on the left.

"Ah, *oui, voila*, this is it," my grandfather announced. We entered the small, dark shop where steam hissed from a hand-held tool. On a wooden form a custom-made hat with a curved brim was being created by a gaunt, dark-haired man. He switched off the steam,

"*Bonjour*, Monsieur, may I help you?"

From the side, a curtain parted and there stood Nadine. Her homework assignment was laid out on the oil-cloth covered table behind her.

"Ah, *bonjour*, Nadine."

"*Bonjour*," she stammered, but remained half-hidden behind the curtain.

Her father asked, "What is this all about then?"

My grandfather introduced himself and explained the purpose of our visit. I caught a glimpse of Nadine's mother through the parted curtain. Turning away as she placed a pot on the stove, she grabbed Nadine by the arm before closing the curtain from the other side. It was then I overheard her father use, the same phrase, "Ah, *non. Non. C'est impossible.*"

"*Tres bien*, Monsieur. *Au revoir*, then. Let us go, *ma petite.*"

Nadine's father turned aside and returned to work. We left the shop and the door closed. His only good-bye was the hissing of steam.

I was told Nadine's parents were fearful and wanted to keep her close by, because she was small and frail. We remained friends, although I found it peculiar that Nadine was never allowed to go on any school outings, to parks or museums.

Nadine was absent the day an impressive, vanilla-colored autobus, with a plush interior, whisked us away for our class excursion to Waterloo. She missed a spectacular day! After more than an hour ride along Chaussée de Charleroi to

Waterloo, we first toured the battlefields, the site of Napoleon's final defeat in June 1815. We went on to the Museum to gaze at skull fragments in a glass case, military buttons, leather pouches, canteens, rifles and even military hats and jackets. In the older, round, panorama building, we studied the circular canvas painting of the battle and admired the Duke of Wellington riding his horse. Dressed in red, he waved his sword as he led his British troops to victory. We bought postcards. After our picnic came the best part. Everyone, including Madame Oudenne and her assistant, climbed over two hundred steps to the top of the monument to see the lion. Could Nadine have managed such an arduous climb? Clambering up all those steps I thought of the determined ladies from the city of Liege, who day after day for three years, starting in 1823, carried baskets filled with earth from nearby battlefields to create this high mound. By 1826, I bet those courageous women must have been really tired and their baskets all worn out. When our tour guide said, "Ah, *oui*, *mesdemoiselles*, the mound is a third of a kilometer wide," I couldn't believe it.

A symbol of the Allied victory over Napoleon, the solitary bronze lion dominated the now hushed battlefields below. He wasn't fierce, but stood alone and weary on his stone pedestal. His front paw resting on a ball, he stared in protective silence toward France. But today, no one was left on these vast desolate plains.

In May, a ceremony was held at school for a former

teacher, Madame Odile Henri Ovart. Apparently, three years ago, she was deported by the Germans to a relocation camp called Bergen-Belsen. We were told that, once there, she became ill and due to severe cold weather died at a hospital before she could return to Belgium and resume her teaching position here at the Lycée. Teachers and some of the older students remembered her.

That Friday in May, all seven grades stood in rows five abreast as the ceremony began. After solemn speeches by Madame la Directrice and three dignitaries from Brussels' City Hall, Madame pulled a cord, unveiling a square, bronze plaque with a cast portrait of Madame Ovart. I was impressed how the sculptor had managed to render her round-rimmed glasses. It was pretty amazing to me. On the plaque it read:

IN MEMORY OF
Mme. ODILE HENRI OVART
1892 – 1945
Bergen-Belsen

As I stood there, I was both sad and puzzled that they didn't take better care of her in Germany when she caught that bad cold. She needed warmer blankets and maybe some Vicks on her chest. That always does it. If she had just stayed in Belgium, she wouldn't have died from a chest cold. Her friends, the other teachers, would have brought her aspirin and perhaps a hot grog and she would still be alive.

I was getting sadder and sadder when the music teacher raised her hands and nodded. That was the awaited signal and we all sang *La Brabançonne*, the Belgian national anthem. The parents who came, as well as a reporter and a photographer from the newspaper who were covering this event, joined us.

A metal stand was set up, and a wreath covered with white roses and gladiolas was brought in. But the wreath was so heavy it took two teachers with the help of one of the dignitaries to secure it. A diagonal purple ribbon with gold lettering was draped across it.

The photographer asked for two students to kneel on either side of wreath. A teacher standing close by signaled two girls to step up: one from the fifth grade, the other was Nadine. The photographer adjusted the pose of both girls then checked his lights.

Abruptly, Nadine's father appeared, pushed the teacher aside, grabbed Nadine by the arm and said, "Ah, non. Non. *C'est impossible!* Not you. Get back in your row."

The teacher dropped her program. Her face flushed. She held her glasses in her hand and waved them in protest.

"Just pick someone else," and he walked away.

The photo appeared the following day in the newspaper with a brief article. It was very exciting. There we stood in rows, two students kneeling by the flowered wreath, and above it the bronze plaque of Madame Ovart. My grandfather cut the article out and we pasted it in my journal.

The students and teachers felt sorry for Nadine after that day and thought her father was mean not to allow her to be in the newspaper photo.

Years later, my grand-père explained why Nadine was not allowed to come over and play, or to be photographed for the newspaper. Nadine was Jewish and had spent the war years in hiding with her parents. But building their new lives, still afraid, they did not trust anyone and refused to take any chances.

Just for The Day
March 1947

Monsieur Jenssen drove an immaculate, midnight-blue 1937 Packard sedan with two jump seats and black rooftop. Its luxurious seats were upholstered in plush grey wool. Two cone-shaped crystal vases, held in chrome brackets, flanked the rear passenger windows.

Now that the war was over and petrol restrictions eased, he and Madame Jenssen often invited my grandparents and me for Saturday rides to the countryside, where we visited castles and historic sites. One Saturday, we even drove to Ostend, and walked along it's windy beach. Three American amphibian boats, left behind after the war, now painted blue, were lined up against the seawall. A placard displayed alongside, offered, "The once in a lifetime ride on our beautiful Mer du Nord for 35 francs." The man in charge called us over and suggested it would be a great unique experience for all, But the grown-ups agreed it was, unfortunately, an exorbitant price. Instead, we walked to the

Madame and Monsieur Jenssen, and their immaculate
midnight-blue 1937 Packard sedan, on an outing.

stand on the boardwalk and ate fresh, salty *crevettes*, tiny shrimps while watching powerful waves of the incoming tide crash below.

During our outings, when Madame Jenssen spotted wild flowers along the road she exclaimed, "Oh look, Franz, they're so beautiful! Please stop. Oh, *oui*, let's bring some home."

"Mais *oui*, you're right, Hélene. *Oui*. I'll pull over, right here."

Madame Jenssen and I ran out into the fields with pairs of scissors kept in the trunk of the car for just that purpose. Stepping over tall grasses, avoiding bumblebees, we cut our flowers. Surrounded by warm, heady, sometimes pungent country air, we enjoyed every breath. Soon we headed back to Brussels with wild flowers in our hair and two bouquets. But, before we reached the city, our day was topped by dinner at a usually, crowded roadside *auberge* where we ordered their *Spécialité du Jour*, real Belgian country food accompanied by a cold pitcher of foamy, Belgian beer. My favorite was *boudins blancs*, sausages, served with sauerkraut and mounds of mashed potatoes.

The Jenssens lived in a two-story house in the Saint Josse section of Brussels. Madame Jenssen was prone to bouts of depression since the night, four years ago, when the bomb fell on her parent's home in Malines. It killed them and her sister instantly and destroyed the street corner. Nothing remained. Time passed, Madame Jenssen began to smile again, but last September, when their son, Fernand enrolled at a school in the far away Ardennnes, the house felt empty, and her depression returned.

When Allied forces took over Germany, the war had decimated the entire country. Its people were broken, lost, and hungry. Too often, overburdened, frightened parents and widowed mothers could not properly provide for their babies' needs. Concerned with this lack of sufficient care and afraid of malnutrition, a program was established by the Red Cross to save needy German infants by placing them with healthy, nurturing families outside of Germany until their own families could manage.

Monsieur and Madame Jenssen heard of this program and wanted to participate. The war had ravaged lives. Perhaps they could heal one of these small innocent war victims. They agreed to take in one of these children for a period of two years. Monsieur Jenssen hoped this would, perhaps, also help his wife.

Wilhem was a pale, scrawny, three-month-old infant when the Red Cross delivered him from the German city of Aachen, to the Jenssens' home in Brussels. At first, he cried all the time, but from the first moment, Madame Jenssen loved and comforted the frightened, blond baby, and called him, "Willie."

For the next twenty-two months, Willie lived with the Jenssens, who cared for, protected, and adored him. During this time, he grew stronger and became a plump, happy toddler. Madame Jenssen loved him so much she wrote a letter to the Red Cross to ask whether she could keep him a while longer. Their short reply was not only negative, but firm, final and included a set date. In two months Wilhem was to return to Germany and re-join his family.

As the date approached, Madame Jenssen became desolate. Each passing day she cried over and over, "*Oh, non, non,* I can't believe the time for our little Willie to go home is growing near!"

Monsieur Jenssen was practical and decided they would drive the approximate two hours to Aachen to return Wilhem, meet his family, and bring additional clothing, toys and food supplies. From then on, he spent a lot of time in his garage, preparing the car.

Three days prior to their departure, Madame Jenssen sobbed, "*Oh,* but I cannot take this trip, Franz. *Oh, non.* You understand, Franz, it makes this final separation too painful for me." She called my mother, "Oh, please, help us! You speak German. Could you go instead, and care for Willie while Franz drives?"

My mother hesitated, then agreed. She hung up the telephone, stood still for a moment, then noticed me drawing, "Oh, why don't you come along, *mon trésor?* Just for the day! *Ah, oui,* you'll sit in the back seat and watch Willie. How exciting! Oh, and just imagine, *chérie,* you'll get to see Germany. Did you know that Emperor Charlemagne's remains and his throne are in the cathedral in Aachen?"

That trip did not have magic nor any appeal for me, although I've admired Charlemagne since I learned in history class about this Frankish King, who, in 800 A.D., ruled the Roman Empire. My mother mentioned our possible visit to the Cathedral to my grandparents and convinced them the trip would prove to be an educational experience for me.

Two days later, at eight o'clock in the morning, the midnight-blue Packard glided to a stop in front of our building. Moments later, we were on our way to Germany.

I sat in the back seat with Willie, who was sleeping on a small make-shift mattress surrounded by pillows. As the Packard sped along, smoothly passing by the farmlands of Belgium, getting closer and closer to the border, I glanced down at Willie and adjusted his blanket. I felt sorry for him. What did his German parents look like? Were they Nazis? What about his new life once away from the loving care of the Jenssens? I was uncomfortable about entering Deutschland, our former enemy. I remembered the war and all my fears returned; the Gestapo, the green Nazi trucks, the menacing guns. I was relieved my mother spoke German, "Maman, is there any danger once we cross the border? Will we see any Nazi soldiers?"

My mother looked back and smiled, "*Oh, mais non, ma chérie.* All that is over, but you'll see American soldiers. They're in charge now."

After a while, Monsieur Jenssen spoke up, "I wonder what *ma chère* Hélene has packed for us today in that wonderful picnic basket of hers?"

I lifted the lid of the deep wicker basket by my feet. Inside were buttered rolls to share, some filled with ham, and some with cheese, all prepared by Madame Jenssen. We drank her light cream coffee from a plaid thermos bottle, the largest I had ever seen. We sampled grapes and sweet mandarin oranges, and best of all, her specialty, the *sablés* cookies, she had baked late last night for our journey. Under the extra napkins, I found the *Côte d'Or* chocolate bar. From the back seat, I exclaimed, "Ah, *oui, c'est formidable!* Hélene really packs a great picnic!"

We stopped once for petrol and after two hours we reached the border. The Belgian customs officials checked our passports, but became suspicious when Monsieur Jenssen handed them the folder with the Red Cross documents. It included Willie's street address in Aachen.

"Everyone get out of the car and go inside." The guard's voice was firm. "*Oui.* Now. Come along." The plain room of the guard house was filled with tobacco and cigarette smoke. There was no place to sit. We stood by one of the four desks while they made several phone calls to the Red Cross to probe this unusual situation and confirm the authenticity of Willie's documents.

"Oh, please, *pardon* Messieurs, is there perhaps a place I could sit with the baby?" my mother asked.

An older guard nodded, and with the smoking pipe clenched between his teeth said, "*Oui,* Madame. You will sit here." He removed the stack of hard-covered files and an opened newspaper from a low, narrow bench near the coal burning stove. Maman gave Willie his bottle and I walked over to look at the map of Belgium. It covered an entire wall. I was impressed. It was new, and showed even more small rivers and towns than the one Madame Clément pulled down for our geography class.

Monsieur Jenssen tapped his left foot and glanced up at the clock every few minutes. When he reached into his pocket, he fumbled and dropped his pack of cigarettes. Three fell out and rolled on the worn floorboards.

"Can I go back outside and stretch my legs a bit?" he asked. The guard agreed. I peered through the window panes as he paced back and forth in the cold, damp air, checking his watch, smoking cigarettes. He shared his pack with the customs agents, then watched while they inspected his car and opened the cartons filled with clothing, toys and food.

"Ah, mais alors, non! Attendez! wait! Here, let me help!" Monsieur Jenssen protested when the agents began to remove the back seat to check for contraband. His face turned red, he tossed away his cigarette, "Mon Dieu! Non, non! But watch the upholstery! Ah, Sapristi! Wait, I'll do it!"

After this unexpected three-hour delay, we were allowed out of Belgium. In less than a minute, we drove three hundred feet to the German border, and stopped at the custom check-point run by the Allied Forces. But, the U.S. Military was as puzzled by the return of this German infant as the Belgian guards, and again we waited. Once our passports and Willie's papers were checked and finally approved, the glossy, white barrier was lifted. I glanced back. Two American guards stared after us. As we drove away, the taller one made a comment, shrugged, then walked back inside the wood barrack. I liked their white gaiters and matching white helmets, but who was "MP"?

"Hitler," Monsieur Jenssen explained, as he turned his big, shiny Packard onto a new road, "was determined to save Aachen, the court city of Charlemagne."

Aachen? City of Charlemagne? Well, since we were headed there I sat up and listened.

"Charlemagne created the First Reich, the Carolingian Empire, and when Hitler created the Third Reich, his plans were to reunite the old, entire Holy Roman Empire. He identified with Charlemagne and that evil monster even fancied himself to be his equal. Ha!"

My mother added, "Oh, and let's not forget! What about Otto Von Bismarck and their Second Reich?" They chuckled.

"Who is Otto, Maman?"

"Oh, it's nothing, *mon trésor*. Now, just listen."

Monsieur Jenssen resumed his story. "Well, at first the Siegfied Line protected the outskirts of the city with minefields, barbed wire, and dragon teeth. The city itself was fortified with forts and bunkers. Hitler ordered a strong defense by the Wehrmacht, and the battle lasted for nineteen days. But even this could not save Aachen."

I wondered how dragons' teeth could help an army, but I was getting too sleepy to ask. I settled back into the plush seat and closed my eyes as Monsieur Jenssen continued his story. "I read that during the last days, Germans hid in sewers and cellars for deadly, surprise attacks on the Americans."

My mother added, "And yet, it was the first German city to fall into Allied hands."

Monsieur Jenssen did not reply. He lit a cigarette and I dozed off.

We reached Aachen just as I woke up. It was a desolate sight. Two years after the war, entire sections of the city remained abandoned. Forgotten. There were no people anywhere. Complete devastation surrounded us. Cocooned inside the safe, powerful automobile, we gazed out upon this eerie, unearthly landscape. Monsieur Jenssen drove slowly with apprehension, until in the distance we saw an emaciated man riding a bicycle. He was fearful, and choosing to ignore us, peddled faster. Our car crept along until we were parallel to him.

My mother rolled down the window. A burst of crisp, cold air filled the car. "*Guten tag,* good day. *Bitte schöne,* please, where is Lindenstrasse?"

The man hesitated, then pointed to the right, "*Ja.* It's the second street, near the church." His frightened eyes darted a furtive glance at the Packard before he rode away. We drove in silence, except for Willie, who needed a diaper change.

My mother whispered, "Oh, but I wonder, do you think perhaps that man purposely misled us?"

Uneven mounds of massive, dark, ancient stones, the bombed remnants of what had once been a church, loomed ahead of us. Only three of its Gothic windows remained. Standing upright, their charred, tortured shapes peered out from beneath this sacred mountain of holy rubble. A single broken arch still reached toward the heavens, pleading for Divine help. But, it was too late.

The man on the bicycle had not lied, for there on the right was Lindenstrasse, or what was left of it. One side of the street was gone. On the other, six or seven row houses were left standing. The utter despair of violent destruction was everywhere. Monsieur Jenssen parked the car and got out.

The house had no number. He found the name on one of the downstairs apartment doorbells, and rang. A tall man wearing German army boots, military trousers with suspenders and a white shirt opened the door, but shielded the young, blonde woman with unkempt, frizzy hair who stood behind him. Monsieur Janssen smiled, introduced himself, and spoke a few words with the man. But, when he returned to the car, his face had changed. Without a word, he picked up Willie, gave us a grim nod, and we followed him inside.

We entered the narrow doorway and stepped into a cold, dark, apartment. We walked in single file down the dank corridor, and passed three closed doors until we reached the last room, a confined kitchen. Here the family, dressed in mourning, was gathered in silence around the coal stove to absorb its meager heat. Mixed with an acrid smell of burning coal, the faint, stagnant odor of boiled turnip, and scorched chicory coffee lingered in the air. The only color in the room was a worn red and white oil cloth on the table. Everything else was brown and tattered.

Five people shared the barren apartment. Willie's mother, the blonde woman, who, despite her worn appearance was quite young, two middle aged aunts, who like herself, were made widows by Hitler's war and their mother, an elderly lady. The man was an uncle — back from the war. He threw some coal in the stove and mumbled in German, "*Ja*, Wilhem's father was nineteen. Killed in battle. *Ja*. Never knew he had a son."

Crowded together, their dark, circled eyes were empty. The war was over, but it had stolen their smiles and replaced them with profound grimness on their faces, then etched it deeper, reaching right into their souls.

Monsieur Jenssen handed the crying boy to his mother. She hesitated, then took him, but did not hug or kiss him. Her aunt understood. She lifted Willie from his mother's arms and shuffled out of the room to change him. Resigned, the young mother followed.

The oldest lady grew tired of standing and sat on a chair in the dim corner. She held her cane in a firm grip and stared into the room. Her grey hair was pulled back in a tight, austere bun, and from time to time her small, pierced gold earrings from long ago, gleamed in the fading light. Another grey-haired woman, one of her daughters, adjusted the older woman's knitted shawl, then reached up to the high, narrow window. She tugged at worn curtains to close them. But, the cruel draft remained, and persisted to torment the threadbare fabric.

Monsieur Jenssen looked at his watch, "I'll go now. *Oui*, I'll go to the car and get the boxes."

Willie returned in the arms of his mother, but wore no diapers. A small towel was placed under his bottom. My mother explained in German, "Wilhem's fresh diapers are there. Yes, there, in his suitcase."

But his mother refused. She shook her head and insisted, "*Nein. Nein. Das ist gut*, No. No. This is fine."

Monsieur Jenssen opened the boxes one by one on the kitchen table. Heads bowed as if they were afraid, the family moved closer, standing in a semi-circle as he produced the items brought from home. Gifts appeared like magic upon the faded oil-cloth: larger booties for next year, a new blue wool coat, and matching knitted hat; and toys: a red ball, a painted wood train, a plush stuffed terrier dog on wheels. Boxes of pablum, farina and small pasta, jars of pureed food prepared by Madame Jenssen, and two thick, wool blankets. But, their deep-set eyes remained void. There was no response from these now, empty human shells.

The great-grandmother, still seated in the corner, was the only one who spoke, "Wilhem," she called in her thick, guttural German voice. The young mother turned. The great-grandmother stroked the top of the boy's blond hair and nodded.

My mother murmured, "I think it's time for us to leave."

As we said, "*Auf wiedersehen*," goodbye, five pairs of hollow eyes stared at my mother's high heeled shoes, her fur-trimmed coat, and her leather purse. The older aunt reached out with her worn, rough hand, "*Schöne*," she hissed and rubbed the sleeve of my coat.

"*Ach, danke*," I said, "but it's just my old coat. *Ja, ja*, my last year's school coat."

She nodded to her sister and whispered, "*Ja, das ist schöne. Zier wolle.*" Yes, that is beautiful. Real wool.

When Monsieur Jenssen kissed Willie goodbye, the child gurgled. He grinned and reached out toward the strong, familiar arms. Monsieur Jenssen's face turned red. He choked, then turned, grabbed the ball from the kitchen table and waved it, allowing the boy to grasp it. He held back a sob, and with his trembling hand took a handkerchief from his breast pocket, walked outside, and started the car. We followed him, and Willie's shrieks were soon drowned out by the sound of the car's powerful motor.

Settled once more in the back seat, I turned around. The lone man stood in front of the house and watched us. He waved once then turned away. It was only then I realized, his right arm was missing.

In silence, Monsieur Jenssen wiped his tears and drove us, in his beautiful 1937 blue Packard, back to Brussels.

Beautiful Shoes
Fall 1947

When I started third grade, my grand-père no longer felt it necessary to escort me to school. I relished my new half-hour walking routine, enjoying the sights I passed four times a day. The shop-lined streets off Boulevard Adolphe Max were my favorites, with interesting window displays in boutiques where I first admired, then made, my imaginary selections.

My teacher this year, Madame Clément, dressed in attractive suits embellished with colorful scarves and coordinated high heels. Because of her fashionable attire, I became intrigued with elegant purses, fancy, high-heeled shoes, the rare platform shoes, and luxurious silk scarves with fanciful designs displayed in the windows of boutiques I passed. Day after day, I admired my chosen ones until, overnight, the display changed. They were gone, and I would start over. If my grades in Flemish were good, I was promised a new purse for Christmas and through the months ahead, I searched for a favorite, waiting for me in one of the window displays.

Walking to school one morning, a section of the side-walk just ahead was roped off. Construction was beginning on one of the row-houses lining this glum Rue du Cirque, forcing me to walk in the middle of this usually deserted street. Workmen unloaded tools and ladders from trucks, while others draped the entire front of the house with an immense, black tarp. From inside, men shouted over the loud construction racket. This lasted for days until, one afternoon, the tarp was gone, revealing the new installation; a glass panel, like a store window. It was so large, it covered the entire ground floor of the house. To the right, a new narrow door, painted a glossy, dark red, was being fitted with an ornate brass handle. How strange. Who would want the front wall of their house made of glass? But, I couldn't see more; a canvas cloth hung inside against the glass. The odors of moist plaster, oil-paint, and turpentine drifted outside. Painters stepped over tarps, scurried in and out.

Once their work was completed, they would pack-up and leave, then I could look inside. It took two weeks until, I was able to use the side-walk again. Inside, the canvas cloth was replaced by opulent, smoke-tone, sheer curtains, draped in graceful folds, held back to one side by a bronze-colored silk rope. The floor, now raised at least a meter and a half above street level, was covered in a plush, carpet. Two small, round tables, were set alongside low, brown velvet tub-style, chairs. It was so dark inside, I could not see more. Besides, I was late for school. Next time, perhaps. But, I would have to wait. Starting tomorrow, we had a week off for school vacation.

On the first day back to school, I passed by, hoping to peek at the odd living room, but instead, today my attention was drawn to beautiful shoes. Yes, because in front of the window sat a lady wearing an attractive dress, but, *oh, la, la,* the shoes she wore were *superbe!* High-heeled platform, green snakeskin with ankle straps; next to her low chair was a small green purse with a gold and emerald clasp. Where had she purchased these exquisite items? She was speaking to another lady standing next to her. Her shoes, also high platforms, were black suede with gold and black bows above her red painted toes. They both seemed so happy and relaxed. I was envious.

It was unfair. They sat, enjoying their day, while I rushed back to school for this afternoon's geography class. In a while, perhaps, they would stroll along the sunny boulevard, wearing their beautiful shoes, browse in shop windows, maybe do a little shopping, even enjoy a cup of dark, hot chocolate at La Dame au Chocolat and share some of those thin, lacy cookies. While this afternoon, I had to learn, then recite, the names of all the major rivers in Belgium. Later, sitting once again in their glass-front living room, they would just relax and enjoy watching rare passersby. And it was right then, I decided, when I grew up, I would be just like them.

That evening, during supper, I shared my hopes and aspirations for a similar, pleasant future. The next day I was happy, yet surprised, when my grandfather met me after school. Following my usual route, we passed by the glass-front house. But the curtains were down. We could see neither the living room, nor the ladies. Never mind, because he insisted meeting me at school again, following afternoon classes. This time, when we walked by, the drapes were drawn to one side. Seated, the ladies were chatting. "Ah, *oui*, Papy. Look. See their beautiful shoes?"

He took a quick glance, but we did not linger. Instead walking faster, he said, "From now on, you will follow a different route, and tomorrow morning, I will show you the new way."

"Oh, but, why? After all this time, why are we changing? Tell me, why?"

"You are to simply follow these new instructions. Period. No further explanation is necessary." That was strange, but I did as I was told.

The new way took longer and made me late, especially in the morning, and I missed seeing the pretty ladies. After two weeks of being admonished by Madame Clément for being tardy, I resumed using my original route and regained the ten minutes, but kept this to myself. All went well for a while, except little by little, things changed in the glass house.

First, two girlfriends, or perhaps their sisters, came by and shared the window seating. They, too, wore beautiful shoes, sometimes satin cocktail dresses, even at lunch time. But now, often smoking cigarettes or filing their red fingernails, their fancy purses by their feet, they seemed bored. Whenever the curtains were pulled back, I slowed down, sometimes pretending to re-tie my shoe lace to get a better look. Until, the day things changed again.

Instead of just beautiful shoes, I saw big shoes. Men's large, black polished shoes, showed from beneath well-creased, "pinks," the dress military pants worn by American Army officers. Today, apparently, the ladies had invited friends over and the smoke-filled living room was crowded, couples dancing, holding each other tight. It must have been someone's birthday. Everybody was drinking champagne, while the smooth melody of an American song drifted outside.

Squatting down, pretending to fix my shoe, I listened but did not understand the words of the lady singer who repeated three words all beginning with Bs. Beeehouissshtd, Baaahdder, Beeeoiouillderd. I enjoyed this unfamiliar American sound, wondering what she was saying. Again, I waited for the refrain, when suddenly, one of the pretty ladies noticed me. Her eyes glared. Holding her champagne glass in one hand, she reached over and in an instant, her red-nailed fingertips released the silk rope. At once, the curtain dropped, putting an abrupt end to my curiosity.

I continued walking to school when it dawned on me, the ladies were probably displeased with my peering into their living-room. I decided, from now on I would walk on the opposite side of the street and pretend this never happened.

Tomorrow, I would take a look in the window of the

taxidermist shop on Rue aux Choux. The boa constrictor looked a bit scary, but it would be an interesting change.

The Flemish Dilemma
Fall 1947 – Spring 1948

My weekly report cards, which I presented every Sunday to my father for his signature, showed good, steady grades in all subjects except Flemish, Belgium's second language. A Dutch dialect, Flemish was spoken fluently by half the population, including most of my classmates. *Hélas,* our household, was French.

None of us understood or spoke the language. Because my contact with Flemish was minimal, my grades in that class were "extremely poor." This created a slight rift with my Belgian paternal grandparents, who stated, "Her poor grades are an offense to her Belgian roots."

A solution was suggested by my French grandparents. "Perhaps you could tutor her in your own language for two hours every Sunday, while she spends the day with you." It lasted only two Sundays. They refused to continue.

"She needs another tutor. Perhaps someone closer to home." From the hallway I overheard, "Unfortunately her mind is apparently not geared to learning the Flemish language."

At supper a few days later, I was told, "Flemish lessons will begin twice a week, from five to six, with Madame Voorkens, who lives downstairs on the second floor."

My heart jumped, "Second floor?" I asked. "Is it the apartment on the left or the right?"

"On the left," grandfather replied.

"Are you sure?"

"Well, of course, *ma petite*, tomorrow I will accompany you for your first lesson."

This seemed bizarre. Often, in the evenings, as I rode the elevator back to "our nest" with a fresh loaf of bread for supper, I caught glimpses of Madame Voorkens on the second-floor landing. Wrapped in a glamorous fur coat, a tall man at her side, they spoke in hushed voices and were going out for the evening. Ah, *quelle élégance!* As the elevator passed the landing, I would peek through the grilled door, to try to see more in the dim light. I sometimes caught a whiff of her heavy perfume, mixed with his cigarette smoke, and wondered what fabulous evening awaited them? At what restaurant would they dine? What theater was their destination? Yanked back to reality, I returned with the fresh bread and stepped into our bright yellow kitchen, to be greeted by my grandmother with her usual, "Very good, *ma chérie*, just in time."

That night, before I drifted off to sleep, I pondered how the elegant Madame Voorkens, who loved fur coats and wore rich perfumes, was selected to become my chosen Flemish tutor in the entire city of Brussels.

The next evening, at precisely five minutes to five, with new hair ribbons on my braids, clutching my Flemish homework and notebook, my grandfather escorted me to the second floor. He rang the doorbell. "*Bonne chance,* and please pay attention," he advised.

The door opened. In front of us stood Madame Voorkens. After a quick presentation to Madame of his *petite fille,* Papy took the elevator back to the tenth floor and left me with Madame.

I was stunned by her close-up appearance. She was quite a tall woman, with beautifully coiffed, dark auburn hair; every curl, every wave in place. Her pale skin was enhanced by make-up and long, false eyelashes. Her arched eyebrows were drawn and artistically accentuated. She wore an opulent, cream color, silk blouse with a flowing bow at the neck, a black, straight wool skirt, black silk stockings and elegant, open-toed, black suede, high-heeled shoes. She put great effort into dressing that way, to resemble a head-mistress, thus befitting her role as my new tutor. As final touches, she had a magnificent diamond brooch pinned on the silk bow and added a pair of extraordinary, large, pearl and diamond earrings. This style of dress continued for all of our lessons.

En tout cas, in any case, that first evening, we sat across from each other at her sleek dark, dining table. A chandelier overhead cast the only light. When I sank into one of the plush, rose velvet, high back chairs, I felt important. I made a mental note to suggest perhaps re-upholstering our set in such a manner.

Madame Voorkens lit a cigarette and our first lesson began. Minutes passed. Slowly she exhaled the smoke, then tilted her head back and blew perfect smoke rings, which floated above her head to linger like multiple halos. Very impressive. Her voice was husky, and her hands were beautiful, with long, manicured nails painted ruby red. Never before had I seen such perfect hands. I wondered about the small triangular scar on her left cheekbone, when she reminded me to pay attention and repeat the Flemish sentence she had just pronounced.

Moments later, I focused on the magnificent, crystal vase in the middle of the table crammed with roses. Long, dark, red roses which filled the room with the most wonderful lush heavy scent. So many roses in a single vase. While reading my Flemish phrases out loud, I tried counting the numbers in my head and was already past twenty-four, when Madame Voorkens asked, "Would you care for a sweet, *ma petite?*"

"Oh, *oui*, Madame," knowing I was breaking the cardinal rule of, "No sweets before supper."

She placed a large, gold box in front of my notebook and said: "*Alors*, choose one," and removed the lid. Rows of identical, large, round, light, coffee-colored candy were nested in pale blue and gold pleated paper cups. Only three spaces were empty. I selected one and bit into it.

Ah, mes amis! Quel délice! The outside was glazed hard sugar with a slight hint of coffee flavor, while the inside was pure, *crème fraiche*, with a sugar-coated walnut in the center. It was called a Manon, and the gentleman I had seen in her company brought her a box every week.

I told her she was very lucky and, having given up on counting the number of roses in the crystal vase, asked, "But, Madame, where did you pick all of these?"

Monsieur Gaston, it seemed, had also brought her these. "Red roses are my favorite flowers," she confided. I was quite impressed. Just at this moment, a clock chimed six times in the salon. Our first lesson was over.

I rode the elevator back upstairs, so fascinated, my head swirled. After supper, I asked my grandfather, "Tell me, Papy, do you blow smoke rings?"

"*Non*, but your father does."

I would have to wait until Sunday to see whether he could. Before I fell asleep, I counted the days until our next Flemish lesson and thought of what a mysterious woman Madame Voorkens was. I also knew she would reach into my mind and help conquer my Flemish dilemma.

One evening Madame paused when she noticed I was staring at her scar.

"Would you perhaps like to know about my scar?" she caressed it lightly with those long beautiful fingers.

I blushed. "Oh, *non, non. Pardon* Madame. *Je m'excuse.*"

"*Très bien. En tout cas*, I will tell anyway," she said

smiling. "But, it will remain our secret, *n'est ce pas?*"

I nodded. She closed her eyes, sat back and lit a cigarette. That evening, for the first time the heavy scent of roses in the room would become oppressive as she shared the mystery of the triangular scar permanently etched into her pale ivory cheekbone.

"You see, *petite*, you probably don't remember this, but during the war, the Nazis sequestered apartments for their own use."

"Oh, *oui* Madame. I do remember. My family worried about that. They even kept me from going out with Juliette for a while."

She blew one of her perfect smoke rings, then continued. "One afternoon, they came here. Banged on my door, and I knew, for you see *petite*, we all knew. *Non, non,* they never rang the bell. They only knew to pummel doors down with their fists. Mignonne, my miniature poodle, ran barking to the door. I opened it and was shoved aside by three Germans. Two were soldiers, the third a Nazi officer. They went through these rooms, opened armoires, ripped apart the bed, pulled drawers out. They left nothing untouched. The officer looked up and down the street below. He took down a painting, studied it by the light, hissed, "*Furshtbar*" awful, then left it by the sofa. Mignonne remained near me trying to protect me, barking at the Nazi officer.

"Control your dog," he warned.

"The soldiers began to ransack the hall closet.

Mignonne left my side. She circled and barked close to them. When one kicked Mignonne, I screamed at the officer standing near me. "*Sales Boches!*" Get out! Get out of Belgium! This is my country. Go back to Hitler and your Germany!"

It happened fast. With full force the officer hit me once. His Nazi military ring caused this scar.

"But, Madame, then — what happened?"

She wiped a tear, then stood. "Ah, you see *petite*, that I will never know."

"But, what —"

I fell and passed out. When I came to they were gone. "So was Mignonne."

Our lessons continued for several months. Eventually, I was invited to sit in her elegant salon, where everything was in perfect order and nothing ever stirred. A sense of great calm and luxury permeated this room, with a matched pair of large, overstuffed chairs, a deep, luxurious, brown velvet sofa with down-filled cushions and of course lush, red roses.

I always left with six Manons, wrapped for me in tissue paper. The next day, I shared my good fortune with my best friend Marie-Anne, and we both walked to school savoring delectable Manons. This continued nearly through the remainder of the school year.

The first time I was shown Madame Voorkens' bedroom, I blurted out, "Oh, but Madame, are you perhaps a movie star, living I in our building incognito?"

She responded with husky laughter. "Ah, *non, non, ma*

petite!"

Her bedroom set was made of dark violet-grained, palixandre wood, with a deep red satin quilted bedcover. Nothing was out of place. Five perfume bottles rested upon a mirrored tray on the dresser, dominated by a round mirror.

That evening, I posed the same question, suggesting that, "Anyone who sleeps on an elevated, three-step platform bed, was either a famous movie star or perhaps from nobility. After all, I saw paintings in museums and a book on Louis XIV at Versailles, and his bed was elevated."

Looks were exchanged, before I was assured three or four times by both my grandparents and my mother, "Ah, *la, la, mais non.* Madame Voorkens is not a movie star nor is she from nobility. *Et voila. Fini. Terminé.*"

Two weeks later, I complimented her on the glamorous fur coats she wore the nights I rode by on the elevator with our loaf of bread. She smiled, thanked me for my compliment, and ventured, "Would you like to see my furs, *ma petite?*" I followed her to her palatial bedroom, where she opened a mirrored armoire. Hung inside were six fur coats. Long ones. Short ones. All were dark furs except for one, which must have been lynx. High above, on a shelf, were fur hats. I remembered one night, as I passed by in the elevator, that a dark fur hat framed her face.

She closed the armoire doors, paused, then she offered *une entente,* a deal. "If you pass your Flemish exam next week, I will allow you to try on all my hats, and your favorite fur coat."

How could I refuse? Although by now, I was resigned to hearing the weekly comment by my Belgian grandparents, "Her head just isn't suited to learning Flemish. Somehow *cet enfant*, this child seems to have a mental block."

We shook hands. Our *entente* was sealed. Determined to give it my best effort, I also prayed every night to pass. I studied the strange nouns, the impossible verbs. And then, Tuesday came. The Flemish exam loomed just hours away. On our way to school, I asked Marie-Anne to help. And she did. While we crossed the bustling Boulevard Emile Jacqmain and Boulevard Adolphe Max, followed by Rue Neuve, and the always nostalgic Place des Martyrs, I recited the Flemish nouns and verbs again and again. Two hours later I passed the exam by one point.

"Ah, *oui, Bravo*. This is a miracle, *ma chérie*," said my grandmother. She immediately called my Belgian grandmother with the happy news. Her reply was a curt "*Très bien*."

Never mind. A promised reward awaited me at Madame Voorkens' apartment. Today was Tuesday, my Flemish lesson was tonight. At ten to five, I washed my face, retied the plaid bows on my braids, grabbed my notebook, and rode the elevator down to the second floor.

I reached for the doorbell, but heard loud voices. Madame Voorkens and Monsieur Gaston's voices sounded angry. There was a crash and I knew it was the crystal vase

School girls and best friends, Marie-Anne and
me in our favorite park.

filled with her favorite roses. My heart raced. I ran up seven or eight stone steps by the landing and crouched down. Suddenly, the door opened and out stormed a furious Monsieur Gaston. He never saw me. He lit a cigarette as he rang for the elevator. I trembled and wanted to be back upstairs in the safety of "our nest." To pretend this had never happened. But I also wanted to see her. I sat on the cold stone steps, waited a few minutes, then rang the doorbell. There was the sound of her footsteps. The door opened, just a little. From behind it, she murmured in her throaty voice, "There will not be our usual lesson, tonight, *ma petite. Je regrette, infiniment.* I am truly sorry."

"Oh Madame, I must tell you I passed my Flemish exam today. *Oui. Grace a vous,* thanks to you, Madame."

Silence was her only reply before the door closed. With the click of the dead-bolt as a final confirmation, I rode the elevator back upstairs. Just as I entered our apartment, the telephone rang. "Madame Voorkens *regrette* but something unexpected has happened, and this evening's lesson will be postponed until Thursday," repeated my puzzled grandmother as she hung up.

That evening, it dawned on me. Marie-Anne and I would never again walk to school savoring Manons, courtesy of Monsieur Gaston. I dismissed thoughts of all those glamorous fur coats and hats. Instead, I gave a profound, silent, *merci* to the beautiful Madame Voorkens. For with her help, I was able to pass the infamous Flemish exam.

The Turquoise Raincoat
Spring 1948

Until the age of eight, I was always dressed in the same dull, wartime colors. Grey, beige, and brown, and was often told by my grandmother, "Red is a vulgar color." Since I wore a Catholic uniform for my first two school years, it left me with an aversion to blues, especially navy blue.

Last summer, I overheard my great-grandmother say, "Oh, but why always dress *cette pauvre enfant*, this poor child, in such somber colors?" And those words remained in my memory.

Today, because I passed my Flemish exam (by one point), and my ninth birthday was just a week away, I was promised a new raincoat as a reward; not one off the rack, but, custom-made. A specialty shop had recently opened in the Galeries Saint-Hubert, where they offered custom-designed raincoats, delivered in four weeks. Disappointed, I would have much preferred selecting one today, from a department store rack. When the eager shopkeeper handed me a folder with colored swatches of beautiful new fabric just imported from *l'Amérique*, I sank into one of the plump leather chairs to glance through the folder.

Never before had I seen such exquisite colors: reds — from vermillion, to crimson, to scarlet, a deep rose, followed by two variations of pink. Of course, always, those obligatory navy and royal blues, two shades of paler blues, and then — all the greens. Here, an unusual color caught my eye, a pale turquoise, more like a sea-foam green, I admired once before in a movie I saw with Papy. The beautiful American movie star, Esther Williams, my goddess, wore a bathing suit in that very shade of turquoise green.

My grandmother exclaimed, "*Non, non.* This color is too impractical. It will get soiled too easily." Unfortunately, my mother agreed.

But I caught the eye of the saleslady who reassured them. "*Ah*, but it can, of course, be sent to the dry cleaners. *Et vraiment*, truly, Mesdames, this unusual turquoise shade enhances the color of your *charmante petite fille's* hair and eyes."

I stared at the color swatch. *Oh, oui, oui.* That's it. Perfect. I closed my eyes, made a wish and it worked! Within moments, the order was placed for a classic trench coat style and a date was set for pick-up.

"*Oui, très bien,* Mesdames. Of course, a matching hat is offered for a small extra sum." The saleslady smiled, as she placed the beige sample on my head. Although the wrong color, my grandmother and mother agreed.

"*Oui. Très bien.* We'll take it too."

It had a soft brim and a strap, very much in the style of the yellow slickers worn by fishermen. In fact, on the small cans of Norwegian sardines which we often ate for supper, the bearded fisherman wore the same hat. However, the back brim of his Norwegian hat was longer, which made perfect sense, since he was out on a fishing boat in the Baltic seas, battling a storm, trying to catch all those slippery sardines for everyone to enjoy with freshly squeezed lemon and buttered, crusty bread.

Four weeks later, Papy and I picked up my new turquoise raincoat and hat. He allowed me to wear them home, though it was a sunny afternoon. For the first time in my life, I felt pretty. I loved the unusual turquoise color, and enjoyed the slight whiffs of this unusual, new fabric sent here all the way from *l'Amérique*, a country so very far away. Pleased, I carried the glossy red bag holding my former coat, while I admired my reflection in store windows we passed along the way, knowing this color held promises of new beginnings. New, wonderful things to come.

Le Soir was my grandfather's late afternoon newspaper. Every evening, before supper, once I finished my homework, I joined Papy in the salon. There, sitting in his leather club-chair reading world news, he waited for me. Once I settled on the wide arm of his chair, he methodically folded the newspaper to the comic strips section.

With gleeful anticipation, we read our two favorites,

"Monsieur Subito" and "Le Petit Roi," the Little King. During our daily evening ritual, we commented and laughed about whatever mischief or troubles these characters found themselves in that day.

But since the purchase of my new raincoat, we added to our ritual. After reading the comic strips, we turned to the weather section to see if the weather predicted for the following day could provide a suitable excuse to wear my new coat. Sometimes, I even prayed that, instead of tomorrow's predicted "sunny day," it would, with Divine Help, turn into: "Rainy day with possible thunderstorms." I wore my turquoise raincoat as often as I could, knowing Esther Williams would not only approve of the color, but should she visit Brussels, she would certainly order the same for herself.

Soon the school year ended. Now that the war was over, and we were able to travel again, we left Brussels for our summer vacation at our family home in Brittany. I was promised by my mother that Brittany was famous for its rain and drizzle. However, my raincoat and hat were packed in my suitcase, since I was told, "Its delicate color could easily get soiled in the various taxis and trains."

Before we boarded the Paris-Brest Express, I looked up at the grey skies of Paris one last time, knowing Brittany would also provide plenty of mist and rain during our summer stay. To make that a bit more certain, as soon as we settled into our window seats, I sent up a little prayer.

Minutes later, as our train pulled away from the Paris-

Montparnasse station, heading toward our destination, teasing raindrops appeared upon the cold window pane.

Une Vraie Ophélie
Summer 1948

Once settled for the summer season in our home in Brittany, a series of obligatory visits to family friends began. I managed to be excused so I could escape to read my new book, or to draw. Sometimes, I visited their gardens, after my promise not to touch or pick flowers.

Soon after our arrival, we were invited up on the hill to Docteur and Madame Barbier for afternoon tea. Just as we left our house my prayers were answered, when a fine Brittany mist began to fall. I was thrilled. I ran upstairs and slipped into my turquoise raincoat and hat. Downstairs, everyone scrambled to find scarves, hats and their favorite umbrellas in the bamboo stand by the front door. Minutes later, my grandparents, my mother, Aunt Yvonne and I, shielded beneath bobbing umbrellas, headed to the Barbier's pink villa.

Their property was shaped in a long triangle, lined on two sides by fifteen-foot-high, vine-covered stone walls. These came to a point where two country roads, which bordered their property, merged into one. From two possible entrances, we always chose the side one, closest to our house. Nestled into this protective, stone wall was a low-arched doorway with tangled, flowered vines, above the faded blue door. It seemed like a secret entrance to another world.

It took two, sometimes three, shoves before its old hinges groaned, and the door edged open. This unpleasant sound was surpassed by the magical notes from a delicate bell attached long ago to the back of the door. I admired this bronze bell with its green patina and thought it much too pretty to be hidden. We climbed five steep, worn, narrow stone steps, to suddenly face an open vista on one of four terraced flower and vegetable gardens, cared for daily by Madame Barbier with the help of Monsieur Morain, their gardener.

Docteur Barbier, a retired pharmacist from Paris, was not only stone deaf but suffered from a serious hunch back. Because he could not hear, he seemed angry and gruff. When I shook his hand to say "*Bonjour*, Docteur," his grip, with those long bony fingers felt strong and scared me. His passions were two. A collection of postcards from around the world, kept in albums, and attached with little black, pre-glued, triangular corner-strips. His second passion was painting. He was very good, I thought, as I studied the work he meticulously copied from art books or his favorite postcards. Once his latest *chef d'oeuvre* was completed, it was sent off to the nearby town of Lamballe to a venerable frame shop where, in a manner consistent with the particular period of his latest work, it was framed.

The five of us, well protected by our umbrellas, arrived at the ground floor of the immense, pink, two-story villa and, as customary, knocked on one of the small, glass panels of the door to the downstairs salon. Madame Barbier greeted us. Her smile and the warmth of her dark-brown eyes reflected genuine happiness at seeing us, especially my grandmother, as they were good friends. As always, she wore a complete, winter-white ensemble, which included stockings and delicate, laced, kid-leather ghillies. Behind her stood Docteur Barbier, still looking dour, and, of course, still deaf, yet he too, was pleased to see us.

The size of the downstairs winter salon was minimal. But, due to the dampness caused by the nearby ocean, it was closed until warmer summer months, when the house was totally opened up. It was only late May, which could still be cool and damp. The space in this confined salon was filled by a round table in the center, which took up a third of the room. It was surrounded by side chairs of different periods and style, while against the back wall, three chairs filled yet more space. Paintings done over the years by Docteur Barbier covered most of the room's deep red felt covered walls.

This year, several of his new works were hung in which he gravitated from his former bucolic landscapes, to depicting bare-breasted women. One showed a small, pretty, green snake, called an asp, slinking down Cleopatra's, exposed, bare breast, ready to perform its deadly mission, while her dark-rimmed eyes were rolled back in anticipation. Her long, disheveled, Egyptian black hair, enhanced the dramatic moment. There were several other new paintings. An erotic one caught my complete attention. It was a profile portrait of Diane de Poitiers, mistress to the French king, Henry II. "Diane," he explained, "was said to have such small, perfect breasts, they each fit perfectly into a champagne glass." This left me puzzled as to why she wanted her breasts in a champagne glass, instead of just slowly sipping and enjoying its bubbles, as we did when we celebrated our birthdays or the New Year. *En tout cas*, I remained fascinated by the details of this lady's anatomy. Docteur Barbier left nothing to the imagination and I could not resist staring at her nipple, which stood erect, touched in a luscious shade of strawberry pink.

My grand-mère soon noticed my fascination, "*Bon, ca suffit,*" well, that's enough, and switched our seats at the round table. With my back to the bare-breasted, Diane de Poitiers, I now stared at paintings of languid cows, chewing their cud among tree-lined green fields, with the obligatory stream running across the landscape. These were obviously his much earlier work. Once seated, I said, "Docteur Barbier, I think your paintings should be shown in museums. Oh, *oui. Absolument.* They are that good."

His wife shouted my message directly in his ear. He smiled, then replied, "*Ah, oui. Merci beaucoup,* Mademoiselle." And on that note, tea was served.

The table was usually covered with an old fashioned,

deep red, heavy cloth with a wide, gold-tasseled border, which hung down to the floor. But today, a shorter, white, embroidered tablecloth was placed over it. This made the room brighter, more alive. The table was set with delicate tea cups, scallop-edged, dessert plates, each with a different flower design in the center, as well as silver spoons, forks, and a set of unusual, sterling serving pieces. When I commented on their ornate beauty, Madame Barbier explained, "Ah, *oui, merci.* They are my favorites and were given to me as a young bride by my mother-in-law." I sat, entranced, by all this visual beauty.

A parade of homemade desserts began to mysteriously appear, presented by a pair of hands through a small doorway leading from the kitchen. Their maid, Marie, was shy and, with true Brittany stubbornness, remained in the safety of the hallway, while she respectfully handed Madame Barbier platters of colorful, dainty, fruit tarts, *petits-fours* and tiny éclairs. *La grande finale* was a majestic cake stand, supporting Madame Barbier's signature cake, her *Gâteau au Beurre.* I knew this was going to be a superb tea party and it was. Madame Barbier, a supreme cook and baker, had once again achieved *a tour de force* with her layered, rich, mocha butter cream cake, with a ground, hazelnut batter, its outside covered with more mocha butter cream and dusted with a topping of crushed hazelnuts.

After I sat for over an hour, enjoying the elegant setting, savoring delectable desserts plus two cups of tea, I noticed the room's window panes were now steamed by our crowded presence.

The conversation turned from favorite places in Paris now forever gone, to reminiscing about family members, friends, or neighbors killed during the war. I felt uneasy. The war ended three years ago. It was springtime and we were alive! When the adults inevitably began to discuss the current European situation, "*Après la guerre*", France's Fourth Republic and the election a year ago of President Vincent Auriol, the time had come to venture my usual, "May I please be excused to play in the garden?" Moments later I stepped outside, dressed in my raincoat and wearing my hat, for it was still lightly drizzling.

With deep breaths, again and again, I inhaled fresh air filled with the stimulating, briny smell of the ocean. I was free to begin my exploration, and started by a visit to the rabbits in their large hutch and a few chickens in the hen house. I found a small branch and tried to chase the rooster to make it crow, but to no avail. I enjoyed a stroll in the vegetable garden, with rows of different varieties of lettuce, just like in our garden. I admired delicate green beans climbing up tall, thin, wooden poles and peeked at melons hidden beneath huge, protective leaves. After I inspected the patch of ripe juicy blackberries and raspberries and sampled a few, I turned away. With a growing, cautious, anticipation, I ascended seven wide stone steps leading up to the next terrace.

The different appearance and complete stillness of this upper level always intrigued me. With a familiar apprehension, I stepped into a secret world. Surrounded by tall, dark clipped hedges, four stone statues of ladies wearing very little, stood on mossy pedestals, from which they ruled this formal terrace. This was their domain. I was the intruder. They did not want me here. Ornate black urns held bright red geraniums. In the terrace center, a rectangular pool framed by a black granite border dominated this silent level's large, open vista.

Madame Barbier had given me a bag of fresh bread crumbs and suggested I feed the carp that lived in the pool. Water lilies covered most of the surface. The water was dark, almost black. I hesitated. Finally, I threw out a handful of crumbs. For a moment, they floated then sank beneath the murky water. I stood perfectly still and watched. There was movement beneath the lily pads. At last, coming to the surface was a red carp, looking for more bread. A pinkish carp followed; I dug more crumbs from the bag and flung them in the pool. More carp appeared. Hungry, they came closer. I was thrilled, until I noticed the pair toward the middle of the pool. Obviously timid, they had not yet managed to have their turn. I felt sorry for them, and tried to get closer. I changed position and, without looking, caught my foot in one of the metal garden chairs near the edge. I tripped. With arms flailing, I flew into the middle of the pool.

Going down, instantly, I knew I had entered another world that was scary, dark, murky, and cold. The complete absence of sound added to my fright. Lily pads, disturbed by my fall, surrounded me with snake-like roots. With silent, menacing strength, they resisted my sudden unwelcome intrusion into their watery realm.

Unable to touch bottom, I kicked up to the top and gulped for air. Only complete stillness and deafening silence of the terraced garden greeted me.

I looked toward the four statues in hope they would react to my life-threatening plight, but they did not. Instead they remained busy at adjusting their scanty garments. No one was near. I was truly on my own. The weight of my clothes began to pull me back down. I fought for my life. I kicked and flailed toward the granite border. It took me several minutes to climb out to safety, as the curved granite edge was smooth and slippery. I reached for the leg of the fallen chair, managed to drag it over the gravel closer to the edge of the pool, and used it for support.

At last I crawled out of the pool. I stood, held on to the top of another garden chair for support, while spitting out green, slimy water. For a few seconds, I rested, realizing I won. I was alive! Filled with immense joy and relief, I ran back along gravel covered alleys as fast as I could to share my good news. It stopped misting, but the sky was dark. My wet shoes made squishy sounds as I ran faster and faster, but nothing else mattered. At last, I reached the glass panel door of the salon, leaned against its narrow doorway, still catching my breath, then politely knocked, before I opened it and stepped into the warm, crowded, red room.

Startled by my sudden entrance, everyone looked up at once, stared with a mixture of both surprise and disgust as I stood there with lily pad roots tangled in my long hair, while my turquoise raincoat, streaked in shades of green and brown, dripped green slime on the Barbier's thick, red, oriental carpet.

Docteur Barbier was the first to speak. "Ah, *oui, une vraie Ophélie.*"

I knew who Ophélie was because my grandparents had an illustrated volume about a prince named Hamlet. His fiancée, Ophélie, unfortunately, drowns herself in a pond. She, however, wore a lovely white dress and white lilies in her long, Danish, blonde hair. All I had were stems and slimy roots from water lilies in my long, Belgian-dark hair, so I did not feel any resemblance.

Towels appeared. Even Marie came out of her kitchen hideaway to help. A borrowed, large, blue wool jacket replaced my raincoat as my grand-mère rushed me down the hill back to our house.

My great-grandmother was in the garden, tending to her roses as we opened the garden gate. She did not approve. "Allowing a child such *liberté* to explore the gardens of Docteur Barbier alone. Without adult supervision." Her critical comment added to the familiar tension between them. At once, I was shampooed, bathed, scrubbed, and given *une bonne friction* with a loofah, generously doused with my grandfather's 4711 Eau de Cologne. This, everyone now back from the

Barbier's exclaimed, was *"Excellent pour la circulation!"* An electric heater was brought in to help dry my long hair, while I was changed into one of my great-grandmother's blue flannel nightgowns.

Papy brought me a hot grog, a rum toddy. "Please drink this at once, *ma petite. Mais oui.* Did you know sailors and sea captains drink that to keep warm during heavy storms?" It tasted awful, but it was hot and heated my insides. I had to repeat three or four times how this incident happened and tried to answer, "Just one more time, if you please. *Oui* explain to us. Exactly how did this happen?" and, "Could you at least tell us why? Why did you not see the chair?" At last, I was tucked into the high sleigh bed in my mother's room, beneath a feather comforter, and as Aunt Yvonne stroked my head, I fell asleep.

The following day, my turquoise raincoat was placed in a box and sent by bus to the best cleaners in Lamballe, Maison Louis Lepoutre established in 1929. Their impressive ad in the telephone book stated: *"Votre Satisfaction est notre Unique Plaisir"* or, "Your Satisfaction is our Sole Pleasure." They returned it five days later with a note, *"Hélas,* regretfully, we are unable to restore your garment to its original turquoise color." The Brittany green slime permanently stained it and, on Tuesday, Marie, on her way to the market, dropped off my hat, apparently retrieved by Monsieur Morain from the pool that morning, perhaps pretending to be a water lily. I never saw my raincoat again.

That September, when we returned to Brussels, as a closure to the "near drowning episode" in the carp-filled pool of the Barbier's, I was enrolled in swimming classes at Le Saint-Sauveur Indoor Pool every Thursday afternoon. Since Esther Williams, was my favorite American movie star, and my grandfather took me to see all of her movies, I liked that idea and chose a turquoise bathing suit like hers. An appointment with an optometrist was also scheduled.

As the new school year began, I reluctantly walked to school wearing my new, round, horn-rimmed glasses, which my grandmother assured me, "Will prevent and protect you from, *ah, la, la,* another calamity, *ma petite chérie!*" I hated my glasses, but did see a lot more!

The Bunker
Summer 1949

After the war, summer began with an exodus from our tenth-floor nest in Brussels to our family home on the Brittany coast. Weeks before our departure, preparations began. Suitcases appeared and were packed methodically, until departure day, when my grandparents and I left for Paris by train. There, we spent two days at Aunt Marcelle's town-house. I liked staying there. She had a small garden in the back with fragrant, pale roses, and a pet, Mathilde, a clever turtle that was great at hiding from me. My three cousins: twelve-year old twins, Jeannine and Jacqueline, and their brother, Claude, fourteen, were amused by the protective, controlled upbringing my grandparents provided.

On our first evening, during supper, my grandmother suggested, "If you're not going to la Côte d'Azur this summer, *ma chére* Marcelle, why don't you come with the children, and spend two weeks with us in Brittany?" Aunt Marcelle accepted, and a date was set.

Three generations of beautiful French women:
my grandmother, Alice, my great-grandmother,
Marie, my mother — and me.

Two days after their arrival in Brittany, I became aware of my cousins' condescending attitude toward me, while often, they reminded me, "We are true Parisians. But, you, you are just *une petite Bruxelloise.*"

Once in bed that night, wounded by their superior attitude, I realized I needed to prove myself. To show them that I, too, knew of interesting things, of places to discover and explore. I would then gain their respect and no longer be treated as just a little runt. In order to achieve this, two possibilities came up.

The first was a little risky, and somewhat scary. Even for me. Named Le Verdelet, the large rock formation, shaped like a pyramid, rose beyond the shore of our crescent-shaped beach. Only accessible at certain low-tides, it provided a great destination for shell-fishing excursions and collect clams, mussels, crayfish, crabs and those tasty *petits bigorneaux,* winkles, later enjoyed once dipped in garlic butter. But, Le Verdelet could be treacherous, for there, the incoming tide was famous for its rolling speed. If trapped, you had to swim back to shore with your clothes on, while holding your pail, and fishing net!

Last summer, I heard of a tragedy, ten years ago, when several English tourists who, ignoring the warnings, had remained too long. Trapped suddenly by the swirling sea, cold and wet, they huddled, clinging into narrow ridges high up on the rock, until dawn. The bravest one who tried to swim back for help, unfortunately drowned before reaching the shore.

Our house in Brittany.

Le Verdelet

This story left me so fearful I only went fishing once to Le Verdelet, with my grand-père. On that day, he tried repeatedly to reassure me by taking a folded tide chart from his pocket then pointing to the hands on his pocket-watch to show me we had plenty of time before the tide returned. Yet, still *affolée*, distracted, I kept looking at the sea in the far-away distance, insisting over and over it was now time for us to leave. We returned with our pails filled with crabs and crayfish which we all enjoyed for supper that night. However, on our way home, I was told, "Ah, *non*! Never again. This is *absolument* the last time, *ma petite*, that you'll come along."

But there was another interesting place I knew. A Nazi bunker. I went there with my grandparents, when cousins Edmond and Blanchette visited from Paris last summer. It was off the main winding road, half-way to the next village of Pléneuf. The uphill road to get there was quite steep.

On this third morning, Claude wore his new sailor cap and announced, "*Alors*, I feel like a walk to the seaport. We'll see real Breton fishing boats. Look inside their lobster traps lined on the docks."

Jeannine squealed, "Oh, *non, non*, Claude. You know how I detest lobsters! They scare me."

I ventured, "Well, I know an interesting place. I could show it to you."

Jacqueline adjusted her barrette, "*Oh, la, la*. Really? *Alors* then, what is it?"

Claude added, "*Oui*. Tell us first. Then we'll decide if

we want to go."

"It's a Nazi bunker."

"You mean a real German bunker?" he exclaimed.

"Oui."

Jacqueline hesitated. "But what if we get lost? Who would come and find us?"

"Oh, I know the way. I've been there many times."

"Ah, ca c'est formidable!" Claude ran, threw open the garden gate and shouted, "Alors, let's go! Allons visiter les Nazis!" Let's visit the Nazis!

I was now in charge. The leader. I knew of a shortcut through the center of town, but to prolong our adventure, I chose to lead them the long way. We began by passing the mysterious Café du Coin, at the end of our street. Its green shutters closed, as always. The owner, Veuve Gérard, remained shunned by the villagers for having entertained Germans during the war. Now a recluse, she lived alone, inside. I saw her one day, watering her plants upstairs on the former café's terrace. Partially hidden by vine covered trellises, dressed in an old bathrobe, her hair unkempt, she ignored me when, walking by, I waved and said, "Bonjour, Madame Gérard."

Following the road along the hill behind our house, we passed by Dr. Barbier's pink villa, continued up the steep, winding road until nearing the top, we turned left to venture upon an uneven rocky path through a wooded area. Minutes later we stood at the edge of a wide vista overlooking undulating green hills, bordered at times by wheat fields. Visible in the distance, was the old village of Pléneuf. Its silhouetted church steeple surrounded by tight clusters of low, stone houses.

It took us over twenty minutes to clamber down the slope, wriggle our way through a wheat field to finally reach that steep road to Pléneuf.

I recognized the farm house on the left, with its stone arch, and low-pitch thatched roof. Somewhere in the barnyard, a rooster crowed. Cows mooed nearby. We passed by, but ran when a sturdy farm dog barked then lunged toward us. Tied by a rope, he could not reach us. When I looked back, the peasant's wife stood at the half-opened Dutch door. Still wiping a bowl, she glanced our way, then yelled at the dog. He obeyed her and turned back.

"Oh, but what smells so bad around here?" asked Jacqueline, holding her nose.

"Ah, oui, it's cow dung. You're now in la vraie campagne, the real countryside."

"Do you know where you're taking us? I don't want to get lost, you know," added Jeannine.

"Oh, don't worry. I know the way. We'll be there soon," I said, while looking for my landmark, the concrete utility pole. Ahead, the road still curved, until, just past the curve, there stood the first pole after the farm. Only three or four meters beyond it, I stopped.

"The bunker is in there."

"Where? I don't see it," said Claude.

With the tips of my espadrilles I kicked back new brush and soon found traces of the path leading to the bunker.

"Just follow me. It's there. Up ahead. Near the edge of the cliff. Overlooking the sea."

But, the twins refused. Scared, they decided to sit and wait for us by the side of the road.

With Claude behind me, I continued through thorny clumps of wild bramble and vines. I followed along remnants of the path leading across the cliff, toward the sea. Suddenly, to my right, wild grasses partially hiding its low entrance, stood the bunker. Its sturdy domed roof still intact. Claude gasped.

"Ah, *Chouette!* Excellent! It's for real! Let's go see!"

We entered the bunker through its single, narrow doorway. It took a few moments for our eyes to adjust from morning sunlight to the dimness inside this confined space. Nothing had changed since last summer.

Built of concrete blocks aligned with precision, these were still held together by impeccable lines of sturdy German mortar. The bunker had enough room for four men, their deadly guns and supplies of ammunition. Within easy reach, a five-foot high ledge, only a foot wide, was built along the entire back wall What did they use it for?

Directly across, a single, horizontal, narrow rectangular opening offered a vast, unobstructed view of the English Channel. But, with sunlight unable to reach inside, an unpleasant dankness remained trapped within the bunker.

This small bunker is similar to the one we visited. You can see part of the horizontal opening on the right. The Nazis had many designs and many sizes, and they were built by forced labor supplied by the Vichy government. These fortifications were part of Hitler's Atlantic Wall, that stretched from the French and Spanish border, all along the sea coast to northern Norway.

It made me feel uneasy.

On the walls crude graffiti remained visible as was the large heart with an arrow, Jean-Luc *et* Marie *pour toujours*, still written inside. Well, that was comforting. This year, they both still loved each other. Various names were scribbled on the walls. Drawn in fading blue, white and red chalk, a French *Croix de Lorraine* still rose above *Vive la France!* In a corner, a black swastika had been painted over with a large red X. But, the paint had dribbled down. It reminded me of blood dripping from a wound, and I turned away.

Claude went outside to explore the hidden bunker's clever construction into the cliff. I walked to the rectangular slit where German guns were once positioned. I stared at the sea and thought of all the bunkers built along our French coasts by the Nazis. Last year, when we were here, my grandfather explained how these sturdy bunkers enabled the Germans to slaughter Allied forces on D-Day as they landed upon our beaches in Normandy.

Five years ago, guns poised, Germans soldiers stood here, watching the sea through this opening. This morning, I stood alone inside the same Nazi bunker. This concrete German killing box, designed to inflict death upon thousands. A chill ran through my body. I stepped back. Eyes closed, I hugged myself.

Claude ran back inside. "Ah, *oui. C'est formidable!* Wait until I tell my friends back in Paris, I was inside a German bunker on the Brittany coast!'

"And will you tell them it was me, your cousin, who brought you here?"

Claude chuckled. "*Ah, non!* Of course, not." He paused, then added, "But, you're a pretty clever girl after all!"

From the side of the road the twins began to repeatedly call our names in unison. Claude shrugged, "Well, we'd better go back." He paused. "You know, sometimes those two are so skittish." Then added, "But not like you, *petite Bruxelloise!*"

"I think I'll stay for a minute. Oh, and Claude, tell your sisters I know a shortcut. We'll use it to go home."

I needed a moment alone to savor my victory.

Les Escargots
Summer 1949

The day after our visit to the bunker, it rained all evening. Claude promised, "*Alors*, if the rain continues until morning, there'll be *escargots* in the garden. Tomorrow we'll have *escargots* races on the terrace."

"*Oh, oui, quelle bonne idée!*" I exclaimed. What a great idea!

The next morning, when the sun re-appeared an hour before lunchtime, Claude was quick to find snails throughout the garden, and sent me, "*vite, vite,*" in search of a container. I ran to the cool, stone-wall larder behind the kitchen, where our cheeses, wines, potatoes, and onions were kept. I climbed on an old chair, and found it, on the top shelf way in the back, a worn, shallow cheese basket waiting to be of service once again.

Claude approved of my selection, and placed the collection of *escargots* in the lidded basket. Just then, from the wide-open dining room window, Aunt Yvonne called, "*Oui. A table, les enfants,* it's noon. Time for *le déjeuner.*"

After we placed a rock on top of the basket and stored it in the shade beneath some shrubs, we ran inside and washed our hands before starting *le déjeuner* with a mound of local, salty *crevettes,* tiny shrimps, served in the sun-filled dining room.

As soon as our plentiful *déjeuner* was over, Aunt Marcelle and Aunt Yvonne, who came every summer from Rome to spend time *en famille,* decided we should leave for the beach, "*Tout de suite,* while the afternoon is young." And our daily journey began. It was a caravan. "What we really need is a camel," observed my grandfather.

The crescent-shaped Brittany beach, a block and a half from our house, could at times turn windy, but our weathered, yellow and white striped beach tent offered us protection. We all wore the popular local blue or white canvas espadrilles. My mother and aunts looked pretty under straw hats trimmed with ribbons or printed chiffon scarves, while my grandmother, her favorite mauve scarf wrapped like a turban, wore dark, round sunglasses. Everyone brought their book or newspaper and carried colorful fabric bags filled with snacks and fruits for mid-afternoon hunger, thermoses of lemonade and, of course, Vichy Mineral Water for Aunt Yvonne, who drank nothing else.

Our afternoon at the beach went well. Our bodies glistened with a *mélange* of sun lotions, as we ran, swam and played volley-ball. Around four-thirty, our content, suntanned,

On one of the balconies of the
Brittany house.

The nearby Port of Dahouët.

lazy caravan meandered home. Supper was not until six-thirty. This gave us enough time for our race. My daily duty was to set the table. That evening, I managed to set the table in less than five minutes before I joined my cousins on the terrace.

Once we thoroughly inspected the numerous *escargots*, we selected our favorites. Claude drew white parallel chalk lines along a section of the long terrace and we chose an individual number. I chose seven, my favorite. Claude marked a seven with blue chalk at the head of my track. All was set.

Everyone held their "champion" snail, Claude counted to three and we deposited our snails within our numbered line. The snails, happy to once again feel "*terra-firma*" took off, slowly of course, but they took off. But all other *escargots* refused to remain in their designated area and began wandering off to the sides. We had time for five races, with Jeannine declared the winner.

From inside, Aunt Marcelle called, "*Alors*, come in, *mes enfants*. Supper will be ready in five minutes. Remember, *mains propres*, clean hands, if you please. All of you. *Vite, vite*."

Claude once again collected our snails and placed them back in the willow basket.

We scattered to different bathrooms to wash our hands before sitting, "A *table*, at *précisement six*." I ran upstairs, Jeannine and Jacqueline ran to the small bathroom off the kitchen, while Claude used my great-grandmother's bathroom in her bedroom suite downstairs.

The dining room clock chimed as we gathered around

the table. In unison, we unrolled starched white napkins from our individual napkin rings. Mine was not monogrammed, but, had a miniature, leaping rabbit, across the top. I enjoyed gazing at him run, and when bored, would twirl it over and over again. I wondered, would he ever reach his destination to perhaps, someday, enjoy a rest? The mood during supper was spirited.

As empty soup bowls were removed, and an interesting assortment of fruits and cheeses placed on the table, my grandfather announced, "Tonight, I am treating everybody to a night at the *cinéma*! Fernandel's latest picture is opening and we need a good laugh."

We all clapped. I ran and kissed him on the cheek. Mamie suggested, "*Alors*, let's quickly have our coffees. We'll save my cherry *clafoutis* for tomorrow." Everyone helped clear the table, and with anticipation, ran to their rooms for jackets and sweaters. In less than fifteen minutes, after we said "*Bonsoir*" to my great-grandmother, the garden gate closed behind us and we headed to the *cinéma*. Excited by this surprise invitation, we no longer thought about *les escargots*.

Fernandel, famous for his shyness and wide toothy grin, was France's favorite comic. It was a great movie. The audience laughed during the entire film. Even my grandmother laughed at Fernandel's antics, although he had never been her favorite.

Afterward, Aunt Marcelle suggested, "Why don't we sit on the terrace at Café de la Mer on the town square and enjoy *un petit déssert?* Perhaps sample their famous Baba au Rhum? *Ce soir,* it will be my treat!"

What an evening we had! We walked home in the dark, each holding a flashlight, we all sang together. The fresh smell of the nearby ocean, only a block away, always excited me. Tonight, it was quite pungent, since it was high-tide. The familiar, rhythmic sound of powerful waves repeatedly crashed, then rolled over high mounds of *gallets,* those smooth rocks protecting the sturdy, granite, sea-wall. It had been a spectacular day!

Back home, after the prolonged nightly ritual of repeated hugs, some kisses interspersed with "*Bonsoir, à demain alors,* until tomorrow then," and the numerous, endless "*Bonne nuit, mes chéris,* sleep well," at times spoken as in a duet, everyone went to their rooms. I fell asleep, still smiling at Fernandel's escapades.

I woke to the sound of a scream from downstairs. The only bedroom downstairs was my great-grandmother's. As a series of piercing screams continued, my grandfather, stood on the landing, and inquired in a deep voice, "*Qui va là?*" Who goes there? Instants later, while tying the belt to his brown wool robe, he descended the wooden, spiral staircase. Mamie warned, "Be careful, *mon cher.* Alex . . . *Mon chéri.*" Since she seldom called my grandfather her *chéri,* I wondered what danger awaited him?

Aunt Marcelle, her eyes puffy, appeared on the narrow landing. Wearing a thick blue robe, her head covered with curlers, she stood brandishing a tennis racket in its wooden press, ready to attack whatever was downstairs. Behind her, in an Italian paisley robe and matching turquoise slippers, stood Aunt Yvonne. For the first time, her thick grey hair, flowed loose. After crossing herself, she, too, apprehensively, descended the staircase. Claude and the twins were also up.

"*Attention*, I'll go first!" Claude exclaimed, "I am a man after all." He rushed past his mother, and grabbed the tennis racket.

It was then we heard my grandfather's horrified voice. "*Ah, la, la – Ah, la, la – Oh, Mon Dieu! Oh, quelle horreur!*" I knew then it must be really bad.

My mother warned, "Please stay in your room. This doesn't concern you," but as she descended the final steps in her pink *peignoir* and pink wedgie slippers, I thought about it. I, too, should be informed of whatever disaster had occurred in my great-grandmother's room. She obviously wasn't dead because she was still screaming. And when the women's voices took up my grandfather's lamentations in perfect unison, as in a tragic Greek chorus of sorts, I too descended the spiral staircase. Pushing the door ajar, I slipped into my great-grandmother's lavender scented bedroom. It really was disgusting.

Every *escargot*, including our individual champions, had escaped from the old cheese basket, slightly visible beneath her bed. They were busy exploring the room, leaving gooey traces of their journey upon the gold *doré* mirror. Some brave ones, having reached the ceiling, were traveling across. Others discovered, then lingered, on the chandelier. A brazen one was perched on the bronze *ormolu* frame holding my great-grandfather's military picture on the mantel. But the absolute horror, was my great-grandmother's lace pillows which showed movement of snails, causing her to wake up in a state of terror.

We began collecting them. Mamie brought a cast-iron pot with a heavy lid from the kitchen, and our *escargots* were deposited in their new habitat. My great-grandmother was led to her blue velvet armchair, while Aunt Marcelle and Aunt Yvonne stripped her bed and brought fresh sheets. Her blankets were carried outside, and new ones brought from upstairs rooms, while my mother consoled my great-grandmother and brought her a cup of hot herbal tea called a *tisane*. Now, everybody wanted a *tisane* to calm their nerves. While everyone was busy, Claude managed to retrieve the half-hidden basket from under the bed. He handed it to me. "Go, go *vite*. Go hide it."

Alas, I wasn't fast enough. From across the room Aunt Yvonne, while sipping her hot *tisane*, asked, "*Mais*, what are you two doing? What is that you're holding, *ma petite?*" In an instant, she plucked the basket from my hands. *Ah oui, mes amis.* Ah yes, my friends, we were cooked. The telltale streaks of our snails were enough evidence. Worst of all, one remained in the basket, *très* content in his *petit coin*, his little corner. Not an exploring type apparently.

They quickly guessed the truth. There was the

evidence. My mother's voice was sharp, "*Et bien*, which one? Which one of you has done *cette chose affreuse?*"

Aunt Yvonne lowered her head. She nodded. "*Ah, oui, les enfants*, we need *une confession immédiatement!*"

My grandmother, her face flushed, insisted, "*Oui. Oh, absolument. Oui. Tout de suite.*" Right now.

My grandfather, arms folded behind his back, paced back and forth, "*Alors, mes enfants*, we are all waiting. We are all listening."

But Claude and I remained silent. The twins had tip-toed upstairs and were back in bed, deep under their covers. They soon were brought back down by Aunt Marcelle. "*Ah, mais oui. Certainement*, I, too, demand *une explication.* Who has been so mean? So cruel?"

For the past year, I read over and over, *Les Trois Mousquetaires.* I knew and admired loyalty. You never, ever, gave up information when it could endanger your companions, "One for all and all for one" was the motto. Our silence lasted two days. Then, Claude confessed. I told him it wasn't really *nécessaire*, but he could not stand being locked in his room any longer. *Ah, oui!* For two, long summer days, we were locked in our individual bedrooms. The twins were separated, a most cruel punishment. My mother addressed me as Mademoiselle when she left my food trays, while our multiple bathroom visits were allowed only with supervision.

On the first day, Aunt Yvonne came to my room, sat on the edge of my bed, and tried to coax a confession. But I did not give in. D'Artagnan, my favorite *Mousquetaire*, would not have either. When she reached for the door, I ventured, "Aunt Yvonne, why don't you undo your *chignon?* You looked so beautiful last night. It will be *superbe* when you go to Mass. With your hair down, you truly look like *une vraic Madonne.*"

She shook her head, "*Merci, petite,* but I can't. It isn't *convenable,* proper," then walked out of the room.

My grandfather secretly brought me the new issue of my favorite children's magazine, *La Semaine de Suzette,* Suzette's Weekly, which I read from beginning to end for those two days.

After Claude's confession, we had to apologize *en groupe* to my great-grandmother, while Aunt Marcelle cried at how cruel we had been and how their father, in Paris, would be "Very, very cross."

Berthe, the surly cleaning woman said, "*Ugh, c'est horrible, et dégôutant!*" probably because she spent two hours scrubbing trails left on the ceiling by our wandering tribe of *escargots.*

We were forgiven, once having gone to confession that Friday and done our proper number of Hail Mary and Our Father prayers. In the meantime, my grandmother took the cast-iron *cocotte,* turned it upside down, and dumped its contents over the stone wall of our courtyard into the stream behind our house. She then, meticulously, bleached it and scoured it, as our regular Sunday chicken was prepared in it.

We spent the rest of their visit going to the beach every

Champion cherry-picker.

day, and played games of hide-and-seek in the garden, which was better than the snail race. Claude taught me to climb the cherry tree and collect cherries for more of my grandmother's famous *clafoutis*. Jacqueline set my hair with Aunt Marcelle's *bigoudis*, hair curlers, so that I looked, "*Très jolie.*"

We saw another film at the *cinéma*, a love story *Bethsabée* with *la belle* French actress Danielle Darrieux. I found it boring, but my mother and my aunts all cried at the end. All three still dabbed their eyes as we walked out through the crowded lobby. It was embarrassing. But once back home, they proclaimed it "*Une splendide histoire d'amour.*" Why was something that made you cry in public be then called *splendide?* I asked my grandmother.

"Oh, *ma petite,* you're too young to understand. *C'est trop compliqué.*" It is too complicated.

Naturellement.

The next day, when I walked to the town square with my cousins to buy some of Madame Tanguy's crêpes, I asked them the same question.

We neared the corner stand, when Claude replied, "*D'accord.* All right. We'll tell you. After we buy our crêpes, I'm too famished to talk to you right now."

Jacqueline added, "*Oui, moi aussi,* me too, but let's eat at the beach. Just wait. We'll tell you then."

Jeannine warned, "At the beach? *Alors,* let's run so they're still warm."

Minutes later, the four of us sat at the edge of the sea

wall, our bronzed, skinny legs, dangled high above the beach. There, once we savored our rolled-up, sugar-sprinkled, crêpes, my cousins described, in juicy detail, their version of the movie's complicated plot starting with beautiful Arabella's past, which led to and explained the fatal knife fight between two captains of the Foreign Legion.

We walked home along the surf, looking for shells and perhaps some crabs, I felt relieved. Last night's movie *Bethsabée*, though not *splendide* for me, now made some sense.

The Bleached Buddha
Fall 1946 – Fall 1949

My grandfather was away on a business trip to Paris when my grandmother decided to go for one of our Saturday promenades for "fresh air and sunshine" to Le Cinquentenaire, a park designed in the formal Seventeenth Century French Garden style. It was in Etterbeck, far from "our nest." The journey started well, and the October sun made its appearance during our walk along formal alleys. But once we headed back to the tramway stop, Lady Rain took over. We ran for cover among imposing old limestone buildings on Avenue Tervueren.

We passed an arched, Art Nouveau doorway. A sign propped outside announced an auction scheduled for two o'clock. The rain now heavier, we ducked inside. My grandmother was thrilled at this unexpected turn of events, as she enjoyed looking at beautiful things.

The room was crowded. On the spur of the moment, my grand-mère walked up to a high counter, signed something, and was given a small white cardboard. We settled into chairs in the back of the room, "*Voila. Très bien.* We'll just sit here until the rain subsides. You'll see, *ma chérie*, you're going to enjoy this. It should be an entertaining new experience for you."

I had my doubts, but preferred sitting inside than walking in the rain. She took a tangerine out of her purse, and peeled it for me. Just then the auction began.

I was short, I could not see very much. Bored, after several yawns, I dozed off, my head upon my grandmother's arm. I woke with a start as her arm waved in the air. She held the white cardboard with the black number 78 on it. Who was she waving to? We knew no one here. Then, she did it again. Blushing, she kept nodding to the man behind a high desk at the front of the room, while holding up the cardboard. This continued four times, until the man hit the top of his desk with a hammer. At once, another man came up to us, stood in the aisle, and handed my grand-mère a pad and a pen. She signed a paper, then blurted out, "We have to go now, *ma chérie.*"

I followed her to a small room. She stepped up to the counter, took out her wallet and counted with great care as she peeled out bills and paid the gentleman. Then she took out her smaller wallet, the one she favored when we went to the market, and took more money from it.

Bored and tired from our earlier walk, I dreaded the long ride home on the tram. A man in a blue smock appeared from the back room, pushing a low, red carpeted cart.

"Congratulations, Madame. Would you like a taxi?"

My grandmother blushed, then nodded. She seemed excited and rather pleased. I stared at what was on the cart. I had never seen anything like it, not even in museums, and definitely not in church. The size of a small child, it was a brown and pale ivory, glazed ceramic statue of a smiling, bald man, sitting. His robe was open and exposed his plump belly. A strand of large, round beads, hung from his neck. Apparently, he was happy and quite at ease. With his broad grin, he appeared to be laughing at all of us standing around him.

A taxi pulled up to the front door. More excited at a ride home in a car than at her purchase, I ran outside, opened the door and snuggled into the plush, wool padded back seat. The auction assistant followed, pushing the cart, while my grandmother searched her purse for some remaining coins for his tip. The driver turned around when the Chinese Buddha was placed on the seat next to me and exclaimed, "Ugh, what is that?" My grandmother ignored his question, settled next to the Buddha, as if he was a new family member, and gave the driver our address.

The attendant said, "Merci, Madame, and congratulations," as he accepted her tip, then closed the door to our taxi. I was thrilled to ride in a car. I loved the comfortable seat and the slight smell of petrol. Once snuggled deep into the seat, the silhouetted chestnut tree tops seemed to be flying by above us. I admired the graceful weaving of our cozy taxi around other cars and trams and hoped the ride would last a long time. It did, for we had traveled all the way across Brussels earlier that day. So, enthralled by the ride, I did not pay much attention to the statue, sitting next to me, but grinning, it too, seemed pleased at the ride.

The taxi driver did not offer any more efforts at conversation during the ride home. My grandmother appeared slightly nervous but remained silent until the taxi pulled up in front of our building.

"*Oui. Très bien. Voila*, here we are. Now *petite*, go upstairs, *immédiatement. Oui, vite, vite.* Tell Juliette to return downstairs with you and bring the envelope with the grocery money. I left it on the kitchen buffet this morning. *Oui*, just go, *vite, vite.* Ah, *la, la!* Hurry! The meter is running."

Once the driver was paid, he carried the statue and placed it on the floor of our elevator. He chuckled and winked at Juliette, "Oh, *Mon Dieu.* Oh, *la, la, et bien*, this one. It's really *très drôle!*"

My grand-mère again chose to ignore him, while Juliette, who devised a plan for bringing the Buddha into "our nest", was busy explaining it to my grandmother who replied, "Ah, *oui*, Juliette. *Une bonne idée.* A solution, *très pratique* indeed."

When the elevator reached our tenth floor, I held the grilled door open while Juliette ran inside and grabbed a blanket. The Buddha once tilted, was then placed on it. Thus,

Our Buddha is still smiling.

he made his grand entrance into our apartment on a thick, folded, pink blanket, being gently dragged and pushed by all three of us. He seemed pleased. We struggled to lift him up and place him on a white towel upon the dining room table, where Juliette dusted him with great care.

"We should enjoy a cup of tea while we admire his new presence in our apartment," announced my grand-mère.

My mother was coming for supper at six. My grandmother was excited to show off her auction acquisition. But, she did not finish her cup of tea. Instead, she opened drawers in her desk, checked contents of several purses in her armoire. She gathered the few coins just found and placed them in the empty white envelope on the kitchen buffet.

That night, we ate supper with the grinning Buddha. He took up a corner of the dining table, while we dined upon the rest. My mother's reaction was guarded. This was unusual for her. At last, she expressed her concern.

"First of all, Papa will not like it, and definitely will object to this surprising extravagance. Second, the fact remains that between the bidding, the expensive, frivolous, taxi ride home and tips, the entire week's grocery budget is now gone in one swoop."

Mamie exclaimed, "*Mon Dieu, ah, la, la,* what to do now?"

My mother used the word *grotesque* several times. I did not know what it meant. But, suspected it was not favorable. After being excused, I ran to my room, opened my *Petit*

Dictionnaire Larousse and looked it up. Unfortunately, I was right. "Very odd or unnatural; fantastically ugly or absurd." This confirmed my mother did not like our new statue.

I returned to the dining room just as my mother handed some francs from her purse to my grandmother, who added them to the coins in the white envelope for tomorrow's food purchases. The Buddha, still grinning, seemed quite content on the table in his new home. His small, pudgy bare feet escaping from beneath the heavy folds of his robe, his elongated earlobes almost two-thirds the length of his face. Oddest of all, were the two aligned dots on his forehead.

For two days, Juliette came to the rescue with her tasty, economical, Belgian soups. The problem was going to be my grandfather's reaction to the Buddha and to my grandmother's extravagance. At my mother's suggestion, they decided to hide the Buddha for a few days, then break the news, once my grandfather settled back from his trip. For four days after my grandfather's return, the Buddha lived beneath the pink blanket in the utility closet, alongside the vacuum cleaner and the dust mop. To be safe, my grandmother placed a collection of dust rags and a few shopping satchels on top. This worked well, since my grandfather rarely went to the utility closet. There did remain the problem of no funds left for this week's food budget.

On Tuesday, the first day of Papy's return, the onion aroma of Juliette's creamy leek soup permeated our apartment and was served for dinner. He ate more bread than usual then asked, "*Alors,* so, is that it for this evening?" Grand-mère promptly served us sardines with a wedge of lemon and more bread. Nothing else. Papy inquired, "Alice, *ma chérie,* perhaps some cheese could now be served?"

Mamie blushed. "*Oh, la, la,* unfortunately, I forgot to put it on this morning's shopping list for Juliette. That is truly a shame." Today was only Tuesday and Saturday was the day my grandfather dispensed the food money for the week.

For the next three days, my grand-mère, with reluctance, used her charge account for the first time and shopped downstairs at the fine Italian gourmet shop of Monsieur and Madame Pasquetto. Located on the ground floor of our building, La Casa Pasquetto offered every Italian delicacy. And they made fresh pasta daily. Their new, gleaming, stainless steel Italian pasta machine produced long strands of various sized spaghetti, handled by tall, dark haired, charming Monsieur Pasquetto, then carefully weighed, and to at last be tenderly wrapped for the waiting customer. A cheerful, quite plump, Madame Pasquetto, her jet-black hair pulled up in an intricately braided chignon on the very top of her head, periodically appeared from the back kitchen where she prepared her daily, fragrant, Italian sauces.

For the next three nights, we ate pasta. On Wednesday, it was served with a thick, aromatic, basil tomato sauce and a parmesan, which, according to Monsieur Pasquetto "arrived *pronto* from Italy, only yesterday morning."

That evening, with unusual flourish, my grandmother

insisted on grating the parmesan, hovering above our individual plates at the dinner table. This was served with an overflowing basket of warm Italian bread, and a spread of garlic butter.

On Thursday, the second night a different, wider pasta was served hiding beneath Madame Pasquetto's famous creamy white sauce, which she called her Primo Alfredo. Once again, our bread basket was filled with Italian bread. For the third and final night, a much finer pasta, called Capellini, Angel Hair, swam in a pungent, garlic and parsley sauce, with small clams, actually quite tiny, prepared that afternoon by a beaming Madame Pasquetto in honor of the required "fish on Friday" dictate. Either the overwhelming scent of garlic or the minuscule size of the *petites* clams is what did it.

My grand-père put his fork down and demanded to know, "Why are we eating pasta every night, as though we are in Italy?" He reminded my grandmother, "This is a French household after all, *ma chère* Alice. Just because your sister Yvonne is married to Tullio and is happy living in Rome, this household should maintain French eating habits."

When my grandmother stood and left the table weeping, I was speechless. My mother came to the rescue, "Ah, *mais*, Papa, you see, during your absence, Maman prepared *une grande surprise* for you, and the moment has arrived to unveil it. So, if you can wait a few minutes, *mon cher* Papa, you will not regret it." Of course, what could he do? My mother closed the double doors between the dining room and the salon then suggested, "Why don't you remain at the table with your grandfather and keep him company?"

I heard Juliette help them lift the Buddha out of his hideaway. All three carried him to the salon. There were murmuring voices and muffled sounds of movement. With all lights turned on, my mother threw the adjoining doors open and exclaimed, "*Voila*, Papa, here's the surprise!"

The pink blanket held center stage, completely hiding the Buddha, now placed against the back wall on top of the large, inlaid chest. My grandfather was invited into the salon to at last unveil *la surprise*. I followed him, with curious anticipation. He was told to remove the blanket and, as he gently did, was confronted by the huge, grinning, statue. The Buddha survived his short isolation period in the utility closet. If anything, his smile seemed wider than before. Papy reeled back and blurted out, "Ah, *mon Dieu!* Oh, my God! It's *absolument horrible*. What can it possibly be? Ah, *la, la* . . . What is it?"

Again, my grandmother burst into tears. She pulled out her handkerchief, when Papy began to laugh, my mother started laughing, and so did Juliette. I did not understand but was surprised when Mamie laughed as well, and at last, so did I. All of us, stood for several seconds in front of the, happy Buddha, lost in contagious laughter. It was wonderful and lasted until, still laughing, my grandmother confessed the reason for the successive pasta suppers.

At once, Papy stopped laughing. "Ah, truly, Alice, *ma*

chérie, that purchase is a folly I find truly excessive."

But my mother suggested, "Papa, don't you see, we haven't laughed like that in a long time? The folly is, perhaps, worth it."

That evening, with the formal entrance of the Buddha into "our nest", he became a member of our household. From then on, he assumed his place in the salon, atop the inlaid chest. When friends came, they enjoyed the story which my grandfather embellished, and everyone took turns rubbing its belly since, they believed, this brought one prosperity and good luck.

ᴄᴏ   ᴄᴏ   ᴄᴏ

All went well in "our nest" until, two years later, Juliette left us to get married and moved back to the countryside. A cleaning woman Madame Broewderer was hired. Unfortunately, she spoke only Flemish but was recommended by a mutual friend as being incredibly talented at cleaning efficiently and thoroughly. For the first few weeks, my grandmother was quite pleased with her skills at banishing dust and dirt. She methodically scoured our bathrooms with so much bleach, the clean, powerful smell lingered for hours, and she often needed to run downstairs to Monsieur Vande Putte's Hardware Store for a new bottle. "Our nest" now acquired a mixed scent of bleach, *encaustic* floor paste and bee's wax. Our furniture, rigorously polished so often, had not only a new, glossy shine, but also exuded the faint, pleasant smell of bee's wax.

But, late one afternoon, as my mother, Mamie and I returned from a shopping trip, I went straight to my room, when I heard Mamie's voice. She sounded upset.

My mother tried to soothe her, while Madame Broewderer explained something in Flemish. I knew it was best to stay in my room, so I did.

That evening, as we sat down to supper, our Buddha looked different, more like a ghost. He was now all white. Gone were the details on his face, the two dots on his forehead, the heavy, beaded necklace, around his short neck. Gone too, were the numerous, intricate, folds of his robe. He was as shiny as our white bathtub.

Silence filled the room as we ate supper that night. It was a bleak, hour long meal. Most unusual, even my mother was silent. Once excused, from my room I overheard bits of conversation as they drank their coffee.

Apparently, this afternoon, Madame Broewderer, used a cleaning rag with a scouring bleaching powder in the bathroom, as she always did, when it occurred to her how much nicer and cleaner the statue of the Buddha in the salon would look if she scrubbed it white as she did our bathtub. She explained it took her almost three hours to achieve this cleaning perfection.

On this glum *soirée*, the Buddha sat staring back at us in its new, blank, white splendor, looking more like a white porcelain sink than an antique Chinese statue.

Madame Broewderer was dismissed the next day. My

grandmother felt her cleaning passions had gone too far and feared her bleaching capabilities might be applied to our other valuable antiques or, "Ah, la, la, Mon Dieu, even, perhaps, to our collection of paintings during our absence."

Since Papy now liked the Buddha, he decided to find an artistic and talented person who would replace the, ivory and brown tones which gave our statue its character. I accompanied him on this quest to several studios that specialized in restorations of paintings. But after my grand-père's detailed descriptions, none would accept our Buddha since he was made of glazed ceramic and not canvas.

One evening, heading home along Rue du Roulean, feeling quite defeated again in our quest, we passed a shop on the corner of Quai au Bois à Brûler, three blocks from our apartment. A black, wood sign hung from a chain above the entrance, said: Framing & Restorations. It sounded promising.

We decided to enter this narrow shop and were greeted by the pungent mixed odor of linseed oil and turpentine. I found this unfamiliar combined smell pleasant and exciting. I stood next to my grandfather, amazed by beautiful frame samples displayed on three walls. The shop's owner, a tall, imposing man with thick red hair and red beard, appeared from behind a heavy draped curtain, which he left partially open. A painting was propped on his large easel while three others were propped on a green, felt-covered table.

An artist, he looked the part with his thick, black wool

turtleneck sweater and typical Belgian dark brown wide-wale corduroy pants held on by a coarse, leather belt. He began by showing my grandfather some of his own paintings, explained that he also did framing and restorations. Perfect. He spoke Flemish better than French, but after a detailed explanation in French by my grand-père, the artist agreed to restore our Buddha. A price was set, and an appointment made for ten o'clock the next morning. He could not leave his shop, however, so we were to bring it. Relieved, we returned home to share the promising news with Mamie.

The next morning, Papy and I left, carrying the Buddha covered once more by the pink blanket. It was quite heavy. There were street benches along the way and we took breaks until we entered the small shop. There was a surprised look on the owner's face when, with relief, we deposited the Buddha on his wooden counter. He did not bond with it, and explained he had no idea it was that size when he gave the quote yesterday. The price had gone up. I remained behind my grandfather, focused at the perfect order in which the frame samples hung upon the walls, hoping he would agree to the new price, because I dreaded having to carry Buddha back home. After three or four minutes, a new price was agreed upon with a promise of a four-week's completion.

Eight weeks later, my grand-mère visited his shop to inquire about the delay. Apparently, he did not quite understand what the final result should look like and lost his nerve, afraid to tackle this bizarre project. He hadn't even started. My grand-mère, with patient persuasion, convinced him otherwise; even chose the color of paint with him. She explained, in great detail, what it had looked like and, once having pumped up his confidence, got a new delivery date.

She then suggested, "I would be so grateful if you would agree to deliver it, as you seem so strong, and, surely, it would be nothing for you to carry this statue only three short blocks. With an added tip, *naturellement*."

He agreed, and two weeks later, on a Saturday at nine in the morning, just after my grandfather left to buy the newspaper, he delivered our Buddha, carried like a baby in his powerful arms. Gently, he placed him back in the salon in his place of honor on the chest. When my beaming grandmother tipped him he was so pleased, and exited with short bows repeating, "*Merci* Madame! *Ah, oui, merci, merci, beaucoup. Au revoir,* Madame."

For several moments, Mamie sat in silence in front of her returned treasure. She then reflected tenderly, "I just don't understand why, but I really like him. Don't you like him, too, *ma chérie?*"

I thought about it, then replied, "He really is quite repulsive looking, but, *moi aussi,* I like him very much." We laughed and hugged. Our grinning Buddha had returned home and once again, all was well in "our nest."

Epilogue

I stood on another continent, sixty years later, on this snowy December afternoon, next to the statue of the grinning Buddha. Beyond him the French doors lead to my seaside garden, now asleep beneath its protective white blanket. Vivaldi's Winter Concerto No.41 was on the radio, and the scent of bayberry wafted through my Cape Cod cottage as I anticipated the arrival of friends for our customary holiday celebration. Suddenly, a rush of immense gratitude filled my heart, sending a shiver through my body, and leaving me with a smile.

I named my cottage *"Mon Réfuge,"* and hung a hand-painted sign on the garden gate. It is surrounded by wildlife. There are no green Nazi trucks here, and only birds, not bombs, fly overhead. When, on early summer dawns the garden calls for my presence, like an offering, the breeze brings me a whiff of the nearby ocean. Grateful, I catch and inhale slowly, again and again, like a long-forgotten perfume of my childhood.

It reminds me of our garden in Brittany. I savor the garden's serenity, and I delight in the familiar sound of bees in fragrant lavender beds. Now and then the scent of roses drifts by. My eyes follow the irregular rock outlines of the flower beds and I am pleased at having recreated this similar haven so many years later, on this side of the Atlantic.

This garden first whispered, then nurtured me, allowing my mind to wander, allowing memories and ghosts of my past to return. At first, like a rare mist from far away, they drifted in, but soon surrounded and beckoned me to follow them on this overdue journey to people and events they wanted me to re-visit. They wanted the pages of my book to speak about that unique period in history. At long last, they danced, ran, laughed, cried and loved in the pages of the memoir I've written. In the solace found in my garden, I finally revisited my childhood. Words flowed as though they had been waiting for my long overdue visit.

These childhood memories are now on pages for others to read and share. Writing them has taken more than eight years as I recalled the war seen through my eyes as a child. After this journey into history, with the writing and completion of these memoirs, I feel not only at peace, but loved. It has been a long voyage.

But for now, it is time to *vite, vite*, greet friends who have arrived for French specialties and a holiday celebration in my new "nest", my cottage by the sea.

Nestled among traditional holiday music, there are a jazz CD or two, in honor of my very special Monsieur Booth, and *naturellement*, many, many candles. He would definitely not only approve, but — insist upon it!

About the author

Françoise Webb is the published author and illustrator of seven children's books that received high praises from the New York Times and other periodicals. She also designed fabrics and wallpaper for her own firm in New York City.

At age twelve, she came to live in the United States with her mother, and for many years enjoyed frequent visits with her grandparents in the cherished family home in Brittany. She has lived on Cape Cod, Massachusetts, for twenty-five years.

Her next book, *Souvenirs of Captivity*, is her translation of the journal her grandfather kept while serving as a French army officer during the First World War.

Her son, his wife, and her three grandchildren live in California.

Made in the USA
Lexington, KY
04 November 2019